THE *ONLY* 127
THINGS YOU NEED

THE *ONLY* 127
THINGS YOU NEED

❦

a guide to life's essentials

DONNA WILKINSON

JEREMY P. TARCHER/PENGUIN
a member of
PENGUIN GROUP (USA) INC.
NEW YORK

JEREMY P. TARCHER / PENGUIN
Published by the Penguin Group
Penguin Group (USA) Inc., 375 Hudson Street, New York, New York 10014, USA ·
Penguin Group (Canada), 90 Eglinton Avenue East, Suite 700, Toronto, Ontario M4P 2Y3,
Canada (a division of Pearson Canada Inc.) · Penguin Books Ltd, 80 Strand, London
WC2R 0RL, England · Penguin Ireland, 25 St Stephen's Green, Dublin 2, Ireland (a division
of Penguin Books Ltd) · Penguin Group (Australia), 250 Camberwell Road, Camberwell,
Victoria 3124, Australia (a division of Pearson Australia Group Pty Ltd) · Penguin Books
India Pvt Ltd, 11 Community Centre, Panchsheel Park, New Delhi—110 017, India ·
Penguin Group (NZ), 67 Apollo Drive, Rosedale, North Shore 0632, New Zealand
(a division of Pearson New Zealand Ltd) · Penguin Books (South Africa) (Pty) Ltd,
24 Sturdee Avenue, Rosebank, Johannesburg 2196, South Africa

Penguin Books Ltd, Registered Offices:
80 Strand, London WC2R 0RL, England

Most Tarcher/Penguin books are available at special quantity discounts for bulk purchase for sales
promotions, premiums, fund-raising, and educational needs. Special books or book excerpts also
can be created to fit specific needs. For details, write Penguin Group (USA) Inc. Special Markets,
375 Hudson Street, New York, NY 10014.

Library of Congress Cataloging-in-Publication Data

Wilkinson, Donna.
The only 127 things you need : a guide to life's essentials / Donna Wilkinson.
p.   cm.
Includes bibliographical references.
ISBN 978-1-58542-681-2
1. Conduct of life.   2. Health.   I. Title.   II. Title: The only one hundred twenty-seven things
you need.
BF637.C5W53   2008   2007048864
646.7—dc22

Printed in the United States of America
1   3   5   7   9   10   8   6   4   2

Book design by Jessica Shatan Heslin / Studio Shatan, Inc.

Acknowledgments

I want to thank the following people for their help, wisdom, inspiration, and encouragement:

My editor, Sara Carder, and my agent, Stephanie Rostan, at Levine Greenberg. Without them, this book never would have become a reality.

My friends and colleagues, especially David Masello, Terry Keaney, Madeline Johnson, Michael Brandow, Anne Edgar, Ellen Fader, Robert Traub, Tracey Harden, Virginia Avent, Alex Ward, George Gustines, Claudia Payne, Eric Wilson, Larry Silver, Joseph Santry, John Webb, Mark Goode, Courtney Woods, Molly Sperret, Betsy Brown, and Gregory St. John.

Richard Zoehrer, for his meticulous charts; Dr. Joyce Brown, president of the Fashion Institute of Technology; and Professor Joanne Arbuckle, dean of the School of Art and Design at the Fashion Institute of Technology.

My family, for their love and support.

Finally, I want to express my deepest gratitude to all the experts mentioned in this book, who so generously shared with me their knowledge and valuable time.

To Ray

Contents

Introduction xiii

1. THE BASICS: A HEALTHY BODY 1

The Stuff of Life: Nutritious Food 5

Why We Need Nutritious Food 6

Essentials: What the Experts Say 8

Perchance to Dream: A Good Night's Sleep 41

The Land of Nod 42

Why We Need a Good Night's Sleep 45

Getting What You Need 47

Essentials: What the Experts Say 49

The Right Moves: Regular Exercise 65

Bodies *Not* in Motion 66

Why We Need Regular Exercise 68

Essentials: What the Experts Say 70

Getting Off on the Right Foot 77

Learning to Stick with It 79

The Big Picture: Overall Wellness 91

Why We Need Overall Wellness 92

An Ounce of Prevention 93

Essentials: What the Experts Say 96

On the Outside: Clothing 125

The Well-Edited Wardrobe for Women 126

Women's Essentials: What the Experts Say 130

Rules to Dress By, According to the Experts 136

The Insiders: Their Top Choices 140

The Well-Edited Wardrobe for Men 143

Men's Essentials: What the Experts Say 144

Rules to Dress By, According to the Experts 151

The Insiders: Their Top Choices 155

A Roof over Your Head: Shelter and Safety 179

Our Other Basic Need: Safety 180

Kitchen Essentials: What the Experts Say 181

Overall Tips from Top Chefs 185

Kitchen Safety Essentials: What the Experts Say 190

Overall Kitchen Safety Tips from the Experts 191

Bathroom Essentials: What the Experts Say 196

Overall Bathroom Tips from the Experts *197*

Bedroom Essentials: What the Experts Say *203*

Overall Bedroom Tips from the Experts *204*

II. THE KEY TO THE KINGDOM:
A HEALTHY MIND 245

Reaching Out: Love and Connection *249*

Why We Need Love and Connection *250*

Essentials: What the Experts Say *251*

**Surviving the Slings and Arrows:
A Sense of Control** *257*

Why We Need a Sense of Control *258*

Essentials: What the Experts Say *260*

Living Consciously: Mindfulness and Acceptance *273*

Why We Need Mindfulness and Acceptance *274*

Essentials: What the Experts Say *278*

Lifting the Fog: The Ability to Be Real *289*

Why We Need to Be Real *290*

Essentials: What the Experts Say *293*

Mind Fitness: Physical and Mental Exercise *301*

Why Our Brains Need Exercise *302*

Essentials: What the Experts Say *305*

III. The Journey Inward: A Healthy Spirit 317

In Harmony: A Sense of Oneness and Connection *321*
Why We Need a Sense of Oneness and Connection *322*
Essentials: What the Experts Say *323*

Still Water: Time for Reflection *337*
Why We Need Time for Reflection *338*
Essentials: What the Experts Say *339*

Profound Reverence: A Sense of Awe and Wonder *345*
Why We Need Awe and Wonder *346*
Essentials: What the Experts Say *348*

Inner Compass: A Sense of Purpose *357*
Why We Need a Sense of Purpose *358*
Essentials: What the Experts Say *359*

Sacred Reminder: Meaningful Ritual *365*
Why We Need Ritual *366*
Essentials: What the Experts Say *367*

Bibliography 373

Introduction

About twenty years ago—on May 15, 1988, to be exact—I cut out a small item from *The New York Times Magazine* called "Fast Fashion for Summer," written by the late Carrie Donovan, the paper's celebrated style doyenne. The item, barely one hundred words, offered tips on buying summer clothing.

"A wardrobe based around three colors works better than one that encompasses the rainbow," wrote Donovan. "Less is more. One dress, one sweater, two pairs of pants, three skirts, a jacket, two shirts, two camisoles and a clutch of T-shirts are plenty for the season and multiple situations."

There it was, all the information I needed, wrapped up in a tidy bow. Over the years, I got a lot of mileage out of that article, as it offered essentials for how to dress well and, more important, how to avoid those expensive fashion blunders that many of us make every season.

A lot of mileage indeed. That modest little item was the

inspiration for this book. Its clarity always has reminded me of a food recipe: Here are the essential ingredients you need, and if you mix them correctly, you'll have style. But, summer fashion aside, I wondered, why couldn't there be a book that listed essentials for many areas of life—from our health to our homes to our personal growth? In recent years much has been written about paring down and reducing clutter in our lives. But how do you pare down if you don't know what the basics are? And how do you know what the basics are when there is so much conflicting information out there?

This book aims to sort it all out. It presents detailed lists of essentials, based on interviews with sixty leading experts in their fields, covering a wide range of human needs: food, sleep, exercise, clothing, shelter and safety, overall wellness, mental health, and spirituality.

What do we really need in life? Many brilliant minds have pondered that question for decades, and there are many theories about it. Perhaps the most famous one was proposed by the psychologist Abraham Maslow, who in 1943 wrote a paper called "A Theory of Human Motivation," in which he outlined a Hierarchy of Needs made up of various levels: the first were physiological (food, sleep, and so on), followed by safety, then social, esteem, and self-actualization needs.

While this book takes into account many of those needs,

it is not a scientific study by any means. It is divided into three sections: Body, Mind, and Spirit. Each section is made up of chapters focusing on a human need—say, exercise or shelter or clothing—with a list of essentials based on the opinions of leading experts, accompanied by text explaining why these essentials are important. For example, in the Body section, there is a chapter on sleep, with a list of essentials about how much sleep we need and how we can make the most of our dream time. In the same section is a chapter on food, also basic to survival, with a list of essentials for maximizing the nutrients in our diet.

Of course, I realize that some categories are much more complex than others. For instance, spirituality is not as tangible as food or clothing and therefore harder to boil down to a list of essentials. Still, that section contains certain fundamentals that will help raise our consciousness and awareness, but they are not necessarily the only way.

This book is a guide to getting down to basics, and it does not have to be read in any specific order. In fact, many essentials overlap. For example, the need for love and social connection is as integral to overall wellness as it is to a healthy mind and spirit. When it comes to body, mind, and spirit, the whole is the sum of its parts. What affects one affects the other.

As you might expect, not every expert shared the same opinions. But I would say that, overall, more were in agreement than disagreement. The lists of essentials were compiled according to majority opinion; if a particular expert felt that one area was more important than another, I quoted him or her only in that section. For instance, in the category of spirituality some experts felt that ritual was essential, while others didn't hold that belief. Each chapter also includes statistical information, including any recent studies.

So, what do we really need? Ultimately, we all want to be happy and healthy, to live a good life. My hope is that, in the following pages, I have provided clear-cut basics to help you get there.

On the subject of basics for living a good life, it's interesting to note that in Carrie Donovan's 1988 fashion piece, perhaps the best nugget of advice was her first sentence: "Keep it simple."

I. THE BASICS: A HEALTHY BODY

Your body is precious.

It is our vehicle for awakening.

Treat it with care.

—THE BUDDHA

What do we need to live a healthy life? It's not an easy question to answer, especially these days, when we get so many mixed messages about what we should and shouldn't do.

To clarify matters, in this section I have focused on each of our basic physiological needs—food and water, sleep, exercise, overall wellness (including lifestyle habits, getting proper medical care, and so on), clothing, and shelter and safety. For each category, I asked a variety of leading experts in their fields to provide answers to such questions as: What are the essentials for a nutritious diet? What are the essentials for a good night's sleep? What are the essentials for overall wellness? I have outlined their answers in clearly defined lists for each subject.

Of course, nothing is black-and-white. We are complex creatures whose physical bodies operate in tandem with our brains. When our physiological needs are not met, it affects the workings of our mind and spirit, and vice versa.

As a result, some essentials that appear in the Body section also appear in the Mind and Spirit sections. For example, exercise not only keeps our bodies in shape, it also benefits our minds by pumping oxygen-rich blood to the brain. And love and connection are as crucial to the health of the body as they are to the health of the mind or spirit.

The essentials for the body are:

Nutritious food

A good night's sleep

Regular exercise

Overall wellness

Clothing

Shelter and safety

The Stuff of Life: Nutritious Food

Let food be thy medicine and medicine be thy food.

—HIPPOCRATES

The maxim "you are what you eat" may be well worn, but more and more research shows that the food we consume has a profound effect on our health, our looks, and our longevity. But with so much contradictory information and so many food choices out there, it can be confusing. What constitutes a healthy diet? According to leading experts, the essential foods for optimum health are:

Whole grains
Vegetables
Fruits
Nuts, seeds, and legumes
Fish, poultry, and eggs

Healthful oils (plant oils like olive oil or flaxseed oil)

Calcium sources (low-fat dairy products or supplements)

Why We Need Nutritious Food

Put simply, food is the fuel that gives us energy to live. The body breaks down food to get critical molecules, called nutrients, which carry out thousands of functions in our cells, like building and maintaining bone, pumping blood, strengthening immunity, healing tissue, and so on. For all of these systems to work properly, the body needs a wide variety of these nutrients—more than fifty—which are classified as proteins, carbohydrates, fats, water, vitamins, and minerals.

When we don't get all of these nutrients in our diet, our bodies can become deficient. "In the extreme, if we are very short of something that's essential, we will develop an illness like scurvy or pellagra and eventually die," says Dr. Walter C. Willett, author of *Eat, Drink, and Be Healthy: The Harvard Medical School Guide to Healthy Eating* and chairman of the department of nutrition at the Harvard School of Public Health. "In less extreme conditions, we may live but still not function optimally. Many different things can go wrong— less energy, birth defects, or serious conditions like cancer or heart disease."

An unhealthy diet is also linked to two scourges of modern life: obesity and diabetes. According to 2003–2004 figures from the Centers for Disease Control and Prevention (CDC), 66.3 percent of Americans are overweight or obese, and the number is rising, especially among children. In addition, the agency says the rate of diabetes has increased 14 percent since 2002. A poor diet also can contribute to gastrointestinal disorders, tooth and gum decay, vision problems, osteoporosis, and possibly even Alzheimer's disease.

The problem: We eat too many of the wrong foods and not enough of the right ones. The CDC reports that the majority of American adults do not eat the recommended five or more servings of fruits and vegetables each day. Many of us lead hectic but sedentary lifestyles. We work hard, take care of our families, and don't always have time to exercise or to prepare nutritious meals. So we often eat what's convenient: processed, prepackaged foods from the supermarket or a fast-food restaurant, usually washed down with sugary beverages—a combination that can be highly caloric and low in nutrients.

So what should we eat? It's not so difficult. "The secret of healthy diets is eating a variety of foods in small amounts," says Marion Nestle, author of *What to Eat* and a professor of nutrition, food studies, and public health at New York University. "If you eat lots of fruits, vegetables, and whole grains, and don't take in too many calories, the rest doesn't matter so much."

To help us understand what we need to eat, Dr. Willett and fellow scientists at the Harvard School of Public Health created the Healthy Eating Pyramid, which offers clear nutritional guidelines. (You may also check www.mypyramid .gov for the Department of Agriculture's revised dietary recommendations.)

Essentials: What the Experts Say

Keep in mind that nutrition is a science that is still evolving, and one size does not fit all. Each person has individual needs based on metabolism, gender, age, size, life phase, and genetics. But, experts say, there are fundamentals for everyone. For optimum health and to maintain ideal weight, you should focus on these essential foods:

Whole grains. Loaded with fiber, vitamins, and minerals, these nutritional stars fall into the category of carbohydrates, which are essential nutrients that give us energy. In whole grains—such as oats, rye, wheat, barley, bulgur, spelt, millet, flax, quinoa, and brown rice—the kernel has been left intact. In other words, the grain has not been altered in any way.

When grains are refined (like those used in some com-

The Healthy Eating Pyramid

From *Eat, Drink, and Be Healthy* by Walter C. Willett, M.D. Copyright © 2001 and 2005 by the President and Fellows of Harvard College. Reprinted with permission of Simon & Schuster Adult Publishing Group.

mercially baked goods), the most nutritious parts (the fiber and bran) are stripped away during the milling process; what's left over is ground into white flour and "enriched" with some of the lost nutrients. Without absorbent fiber, refined grains are converted more rapidly into glucose, which raises blood sugar. Therefore they are less filling than whole grains, so we tend to eat more of them. In addition, commercial foods with refined grains tend to be prepared with more salt, sugar, and trans fat.

"In general, at least up until recently, the more processed the food, the higher the calories," says Elizabeth Somer, a registered dietician, frequent contributor on the *Today* show, and author of *Age-Proof Your Body* and *10 Habits That Mess Up a Woman's Diet*.

By contrast, whole grains are low in calories and satisfying. One of the reasons is fiber. It slows absorption, so food is digested more slowly; this helps maintain blood sugar levels and gives a feeling of fullness, which is helpful in weight control. "Fiber-rich foods fill us up before they fill us out, so we tend to push back from the table and not eat as much as we would if they were refined grains," says Somer.

Fiber-rich foods also help maintain a healthy digestive tract. "For women, fiber is important around the time of their menstruation, when they might feel a little constipated," says Bonnie Taub-Dix, a registered dietician and spokesperson for the American Dietetic Association.

Vegetables. Vegetables are another category of superstars in the healthy food chain because they are rich in vitamins, minerals, and fiber. How important are they in your diet? "I consider vegetables to be the center of the plate," says Dr. Meir J. Stampfer, editor of Harvard Health Publications' *Vitamins and Minerals: What You Need to Know,* a professor of epidemiology and nutrition at the Harvard School of Public Health, and author of more than seven hundred scientific publications. "They should be what most meals revolve around."

Vegetables are packed with antioxidants and phytochemicals (such as flavonoids, polyphenols, and carotenes), which are chemical compounds with beneficial health effects, such as lowering the risk of heart disease, stroke, certain cancers, and other illnesses. They also contain lots of fiber, which promotes digestive health. When buying vegetables, experts say, go for bright, deep colors—oranges, yellows, reds, and leafy dark greens—because they have the highest concentrations of antioxidants and carotenes.

How many vegetables should you eat daily? "The more a person eats the better," Elizabeth Somer says. "There's no upper limit here, but there is a bottom limit—never less than five." As far as vegetable consumption goes, the news is not good. A 2007 report from the CDC says the majority of Americans do not get the recommended amounts. According to the survey, only 27 percent of adults are eating three or more vegetables a day.

Americans, says Dr. Willett, do not get enough of the

green stuff. "Almost half the population eats almost no dark leafy green vegetables," he says. "That's one area people need to pay particular attention to." Do vegetables have to be fresh to be nutritious? Not necessarily, Dr. Willett says. "Frozen vegetables are often just as good, sometimes better nutritionally because they're frozen very quickly after they're picked. And rather than have something that's been shipped around for weeks and sitting on shelves or refrigerators for another week or two, frozen will often have better nutritional value." (Worried about pesticides? See "Organic Versus Conventional?" page 31.)

Fruits. Like vegetables, fruits are also nutritional powerhouses packed with vitamins, minerals, and fiber—as well as health-promoting substances such as antioxidants and phytochemicals. Best of all, aside from being good for you, they're sweet, refreshing, and tasty. Again, experts say, go for the bright or deep-dark colors: blueberries, citrus, melons, kiwis, cherries, plums, and red grapes, for example.

Fresh is best, but frozen can be healthful, too, according to Dr. Willett. Most nutrients are preserved when fruit is frozen, but some may be lost when fruit is canned or dried. And there is the sugar factor. "You need a variety, but you do have to remember, and that's why we put a limit on the fruits, you can consume too many," Dr. Willett says. Be cautious with canned fruit because it may be packed in sugary syrup, and dried fruit is sticky, which can promote tooth decay. Still, the health benefits from eating any kind of fruit far outweigh the downsides.

Nuts, seeds, and legumes. These foods are great sources of heart-healthy fat, protein, vitamins, potassium, and fiber. Nuts, such as almonds, walnuts, hazelnuts, and pistachios, and seeds, such as pumpkin and sunflower, contain vitamin E, magnesium and potassium, as well as cholesterol-lowering "good," or unsaturated fats, which may reduce your risk of heart disease and other illnesses. But if you're weight conscious, don't overdo it— just a quarter cup of chopped walnuts has about 20 grams of fat and 200 calories, so limit your consumption to about an ounce a day.

Feel free to load up on legumes—such as black beans, kidney beans, chickpeas, cranberry beans, and lentils—which are rich in protein, iron, and B-complex vitamins but low in fat and calories. "Because legumes are high in fiber and water, they tend to fill you up so you're less likely to overeat. They're great for weight management and weight control," Somer says.

Fish, poultry, and eggs. All of these foods are good sources of protein. Fish is a critical component of a well-balanced diet—especially oily varieties like salmon, which contain nutrients like the B vitamins and heart-healthy omega-3 fatty acids. *Safety note:* Some fish may contain mercury and other contaminants, including PCBs, which can be harmful to a developing fetus or a young child. The Environmental Protection Agency recommends that young children and women who are pregnant, nursing, or trying to get pregnant avoid eating shark, swordfish, king mackerel, and tilefish. (For more information on all seafood safety, check out the following websites: www.epa.gov/waterscience/fish, www.audubon.org (click on "Audubon at Home"), www.oceansalive.org, and www.blueocean .org/seafood.)

Poultry (chicken and turkey) is a good source of lean protein—depending on how you eat it, of course. "Stick to the white meat and take the skin off," says Somer. And don't deep-fry it, which ups the fat ante. "Bake it or broil it, anything that doesn't require using fat." *Safety note:* Poultry and fish can be susceptible to bacteria such as salmonella. When preparing, don't let the raw juices come in contact with other food. (For more information, see "Food Prep

Basics" in "A Roof over Your Head: Shelter and Safety," page 179.)

Once standard in a healthy breakfast, eggs fell from grace in the past few decades, because of the high cholesterol levels in their yolks. But in recent years their reputation as a wholesome food has been restored—and with reason. Eggs are a good source of protein, and contain nutrients such as vitamins A and B_{12} and minerals such as iron and zinc. If you are a healthy person, experts say, eating a moderate amount of eggs (even one a day) is fine. But, says Dr. Stampfer of the Harvard School of Public Health, "For people with diabetes or those with a high risk for diabetes, or those with cholesterol problems, I think there is sufficient evidence to be very cautious about eating eggs." *Safety note:* Eggs occasionally may be contaminated with salmonella bacteria, so cook them thoroughly and avoid eating raw or partially cooked eggs.

Healthy oils. Fats are another food group that has been vilified in past years, but they are a fundamental component of a healthy diet. They provide energy, make food tastier, and give a feeling of fullness because they are digested slowly. Among other things, they are essential for vitamin absorption and for keeping eyes, skin, bones, and blood healthy. But not all fats are created equal.

Unsaturated fats (or "good" fats)—found in plant oils—include olive, canola, and flaxseed oils (called monounsaturated)—help lower blood cholesterol levels, reducing the risk of heart disease and stroke. Saturated fats (or "bad" fats)—found in animal products like butter and red meat—and trans fats—found in synthetic hydrogenated oils used in many processed foods—raise blood cholesterol levels, increasing the risk of heart disease, stroke, and certain cancers. So, experts say, try to get all your dietary fat from unsaturated types of fats.

Of course, even good fats are high in calories, so don't overdo it. "When the message came across, 'Don't worry about the amount of fat as long as you're eating olive oil and good fats,' everybody started adding fat back into their diet and the weight still didn't come down," says Bonnie Taub-Dix. "So you still have to watch your calories."

Calcium sources. Calcium is an essential mineral for building and maintaining strong bones and teeth. Other important parts of the bone-building equation: vitamin D, which is needed to absorb calcium; vitamin K (from greens); protein, potassium, and other nutrients; regular weight-bearing exercise; and, for women, estrogen, which helps the body metabolize calcium.

As women hit midlife, they begin to lose estrogen, making it more difficult for their bodies to absorb calcium. After menopause, hormone levels drop significantly, weakening bones and putting women at risk for fractures and osteoporosis. According to the National Osteoporosis Foundation, women can lose up to 20 percent of their bone mass in the five to seven years after menopause.

But osteoporosis is not just a woman's disease. As men get older, they also have trouble absorbing calcium, and they can experience bone loss, too, though at a slower pace than women. (The causes of osteoporosis may be related to a number of factors, according to the National Institutes of Health: hormones, lifestyle choices like smoking, or taking certain medications.)

"Men are also at risk for osteoporosis," says Bonnie Taub-Dix. "Bone health has really been played up for women because they are more prone to rapid bone loss during menopause, but men are not immune from these problems." That fact, she says, "hasn't been publicized enough." The National Osteoporosis Foundation says about 10 million

Americans have the disease—of that number, 8 million are women and 2 million are men. The foundation estimates that about 34 million more Americans have low bone mass, which increases their risk for the disease.

Having strong bones becomes increasingly important as we age, especially because we are all living longer and need to maintain maximum mobility. According to the National Osteoporosis Foundation, one in five older patients who have hip fractures ends up in a nursing home.

Current calcium recommendations in the United States are 1,000 milligrams a day for women and men ages nineteen to fifty (1,200 to 1,500 milligrams for women who are pregnant or nursing), and 1,200 milligrams a day for women and men over fifty. Most Americans fall short of those numbers.

How can we get more calcium in our diet? One of the easiest ways is through milk and other dairy products (one cup of plain yogurt has about 450 milligrams of calcium and one cup of milk has about 300 milligrams). Current USDA recommendations for women and men ages nineteen to fifty-one-plus are three cups of milk products a day. If you consume dairy products, choose nonfat or low-fat varieties because whole milk is high in calories and has saturated fat.

Milk products may cause digestive problems in some people. About 70 percent of the world's adult population is lactose intolerant, which means they cannot easily digest lactose, the sugar found in milk products. If you have this problem, try lactose-free dairy products.

Though the USDA recommends three cups of milk a day, Dr. Stampfer of Harvard says you should try to get calcium from a variety of food sources.

"It's not that dairy products should be avoided, but this idea that women should have copious amounts of dairy products—there's no evidence to show that women who are eating dairy at that level have any better health outcomes than women who have it sparingly," Dr. Stampfer says. "You have to have calcium, it's essential. I think it's fine to get some from dairy, but I certainly wouldn't recommend three glasses of milk a day."

Other than dairy, calcium can be found in certain breakfast cereals; tofu; dark leafy greens, such as collard greens, kale, and spinach; calcium-fortified orange juice and soy milk; canned salmon, sardines, and anchovies with bones; and oranges.

If you don't get enough calcium from food, you will need to take a supplement with vitamin D (for calcium absorption). In 2006, the Women's Health Initiative at the National

Institutes of Health released the results of a major clinical trial studying the effect of calcium and vitamin D supplements on bone health in postmenopausal women. The study—in which 36,282 women, ages fifty to seventy-nine, participated—found that supplementation provided "a modest benefit" in preserving bone mass and preventing hip fractures, particularly in women over sixty. The only side effect was a 17 percent increase in the risk of kidney stones.

The most common types of supplements are calcium citrate and calcium carbonate; make sure yours contains vitamin D. Be aware that too much salt and some prescription medications may interfere with calcium absorption.

Should men take supplements? Men's health experts say it is not an easy answer. "It's a very complex issue, and it's really a work in progress," says Dr. Harvey B. Simon, editor in chief of the *Harvard Men's Health Watch*, associate professor of medicine at Harvard Medical School, and author of *The No Sweat Exercise Plan: Lose Weight, Get Healthy and Live Longer.* "We have controversial evidence that calcium supplements will help women, and much less evidence that they will help men. Now, can it hurt men? Well, in the Women's Health Initiative, women taking supplements did have a slightly increased risk of kidney stones, and since men are at higher risk of kidney stones than women, particularly those who've had stones or have a family history of them, that's one potential worry. The other worry is based on a couple of Harvard studies and some corroborative studies suggesting that a very high intake of calcium might increase the risk for aggressive prostate cancer. However, there are some studies that disagree."

What does Dr. Simon recommend? While men need this essential mineral, they should not go overboard: "I would say that total intake of calcium—that is, food or supplements—should not exceed 1,200 milligrams a day."

Multiple vitamins. Eating a well-balanced diet of natural (that is, unprocessed and unrefined) foods is the best way to get your nutrients, but in an imperfect world we don't always get all that we need. A good multivitamin, some experts say, can provide a kind of backup. "I look at a multivitamin as an insurance policy, because no matter how good your diet is, it isn't easy to get everything you need every single day," says Bonnie Taub-Dix of the American Dietetic Association.

But don't overdo it. Some research has shown that excessive amounts may be harmful, especially for men. A 2007 study published in the *Journal of the National Cancer Institute* found that men who took multivitamins more than once a day were 32 percent more likely to develop advanced prostate cancer. (Though more stories are needed, men should consult their doctors on this issue.)

Because vitamins are largely unregulated, be certain that you get what you pay for. Experts say to stick with well-known brands sold by reputable stores. In a January 2007 study, ConsumerLab.com, a company in New York that evaluates health products, tested twenty-one brands of multivitamins—they found that only ten met the claims on their labels, and one product was contaminated with lead. As far as taking other supplements, check with your doctor first (pregnant women have specific nutritional needs).

Be wary of herbals. "Stay away from them," cautions Dr. Stampfer. "A lot of people have the idea, 'Well it's an herb, it can't be harmful.' But that's just not true. Tobacco is an herb, hemlock is an herb. There are plenty of herbs loaded with bad stuff so we can't just assume that they're benign. I think they should be treated just like drugs."

{a nutrition primer}

To stay healthy, our bodies need more than fifty nutrients, which are chemical compounds known as proteins, carbohydrates, fats, water, vitamins, and minerals. Proteins, carbohydrates, fats, and water are called macronutrients because they supply energy, are essential to survival, and the body requires large amounts (measured in grams) to function. Vitamins and minerals are called micronutrients because we need smaller amounts of them (measured in micrograms). Here's why we need them:

Proteins. Composed of molecules called amino acids, which are the building blocks of life, proteins play a major role in every cell in the body. Among other things, they are essential for building and repairing bones, skin, muscles, and tissue; assisting in digestion; strengthening the immune system; and producing antibodies and hormones. Proteins are found in animal-based foods, such as meat, fish, milk, cheese, yogurt, and butter, and in plant-based foods, such as grains, nuts, and legumes.

Animal protein is considered a complete protein because it furnishes all the essential amino acids; plant protein (except soy) is considered an incomplete protein because it does not provide all the essential amino acids, but combining plant sources—say, a grain with a legume—will provide complete protein.

Carbohydrates. Derived mostly from plants, carbohydrates are essential nutrients that give us fuel to live. Carbs are found in a wide variety of foods—from refined table sugar (known as simple carbs) to nutritious whole grains, vegetables, fruits, and legumes (known as complex carbs).

Unfortunately, carbohydrates have been maligned over the last decade because they are believed to elevate blood sugar levels, which can contribute to increasing the risk of diabetes and obesity.

That is not true of all carbs, though. Here's why: Carbs are broken down by the body into sugar, which is converted to glucose. But not all carbohydrates are converted into glucose at the same rate. Some are digested more slowly or more rapidly than others. This measurement of how fast or how slowly food is converted to sugar in the bloodstream is called the glycemic index.

Nutrition experts say foods with a high glycemic index, such as refined grains (as in commercially baked cookies and cakes), are converted rapidly to glucose, causing a sharp rise in blood sugar; one of the reasons for this is that highly processed foods lack fiber. Foods with a low glycemic index, such as fiber-rich whole grains, fruits, vegetables, and legumes, are digested more slowly. They regulate blood sugar, give a feeling of fullness, and provide energy for a longer stretch.

"Refined carbohydrates may raise your blood sugar level, and you could get those highs and lows, where you initially feel good and then you sort of crash," says Bonnie Taub-Dix, spokesperson for the American Dietetic Association. "Complex carbohydrates elevate serotonin levels and make you feel good without the roller-coaster effect, especially if they're taken at the same time with some protein."

Fats. Once a dirty word, fats are a fundamental part of a good diet. They provide energy, make food tasty, and give a feeling of satiety because they are digested at a slower rate than proteins and carbohydrates. Among other benefits, fats are essential for vitamin absorption and for keeping eyes, skin, bones, and blood healthy; they also insulate the body and maintain a normal temperature.

But not all fats are the same—unsaturated, also known as good fats, lower cholesterol levels and reduce the risk of heart disease and stroke; and saturated, also known as bad fats, elevate artery-blocking cholesterol levels. Unsaturated fats are found in plants and fish and are liquid at room temperature; and are either monounsaturated (such as olive oil and canola oil) or polyunsaturated (such as corn oil and safflower oil). Saturated fats (found in foods such as butter, cheese, and red meat) are mostly derived from animals and are solid at room temperature. A third category, trans-fatty acids, found in hydrogenated oils (such as margarine and vegetable shortening), are used in commercially processed foods. Nutrition experts say monounsaturated fats are best, saturated fats should be used sparingly, and trans-fatty acids should always be avoided.

Water. Water is truly the substance of life—without it we can survive just a few days. Every cell in the body needs water to function. It is essential for just about every process—from eliminating waste to carrying nutrients. But how much do we need? Experts say that on average, an adult needs about eight glasses a day (more if the weather is warm or you're exercising). But that doesn't mean you have to sit down and drink eight glasses. You get water from many sources: vegetables and fruits and many beverages (though caffeinated drinks will dehydrate you). The important thing is to stay hydrated. The telltale sign: "If your urine is pale yellow, you're doing fine," says Elizabeth Somer, frequent contributor to the *Today* show and author of *Age-Proof Your Body* and *10 Habits That Mess Up a Woman's Diet.* "But if it's bright yellow, you're dehydrated."

Bonnie Taub-Dix cautions about drinking sugary beverages like soda as well as fancy creamy coffees because liquid calories will pack on the pounds. If you don't like plain water, she suggests jazzing it up with lemon or lime or with a splash of juice.

Vitamins. There are thirteen chemical substances that are vital to human health, categorized by how they are absorbed into the body. Water-soluble vitamins, which travel easily through the bloodstream, include vitamin C and the B vitamins (biotin, folic acid, niacin, pantothenic acid, riboflavin, thiamin, vitamin B_6, and vitamin B_{12}). They have many functions, but one of their primary roles is to convert energy from food. Fat-soluble vitamins—A, D, E, and K—need to be combined with a protein to get into the bloodstream; they are then stored in fat cells and the liver. They also have many functions, among them promoting bone growth and protecting vision.

Minerals. Minerals are inorganic substances found in the soil that the body absorbs through the plants and animals we eat and the liquids we drink. Like vitamins, they assist in many vital functions, among them bone building and maintaining the proper balance of fluids. For good health, we need adequate amounts of sixteen minerals:

calcium, magnesium, and phosphorus (known as macrominerals because they are needed in large amounts); chromium, copper, fluoride, iodine, iron, manganese, molybdenum, selenium, zinc, and sulfur (known as microminerals or trace minerals); and chloride, potassium, and sodium (known as electrolytes). ☕

{sorting fact from fiction}

Every day, it seems, another nutrition guru is touting the next big diet. Or there's yet another study about something we should or should not be eating. How do you make sense of it all?

"Basically, if it sounds too good to be true, then it is," says Elizabeth Somer, a registered dietician, frequent contributor to the *Today* show, and author of *Age-Proof Your Body* and *10 Habits That Mess Up a Woman's Diet*. "When it comes to nutrition and weight loss, the diet habits that work best are based on good solid common sense. Eat your colorful fruits and vegetables. That's the most important thing you can do for your weight and your health. There is no quick fix."

As far as which studies to believe, that's a difficult question to answer. Nutrition is not a black-and-white science, says Dr. Meir J. Stampfer, the editor of Harvard Health Publications' *Vitamins and Minerals: What You Need to Know,* a professor of epidemiology and nutrition at the Harvard School of Public Health, and author of more than seven hundred scientific publications. "People want simple answers, yes and no, but in fact for most things it's not simple," he says. "I think they should bear in mind: How strong is the evidence? Is this from a study in whole organisms or in a test tube? Is it animals or humans? Is it long term or short term?"

Somer adds, "You will always find numerous studies to support any claim that you want to make. You must look at where the weight of the evidence lies. Are there five or six studies or are there hundreds of studies? One study is only a thread in a tapestry. What does the tapestry say?"

So it's wise to have a healthy skepticism, she says,

no matter where you've heard the news. "Don't believe it even if you've heard it on television, because they typically report on one study. They never put one study into perspective. The media reports where the controversy is rather than reporting on where the researchers agree." ☑

{organic versus conventional?}

Concerned about pesticides? Organically grown foods, now widely available in mainstream supermarkets, are produced through natural farming methods that do not use chemicals or additives and replenish nutrients to the soil. But organic can be expensive—often twice as much as conventional. While organic produce is more protective of the environment, is it more nutritious than conventional produce?

"If you can afford organic, that's fine, but the evidence that there's an important advantage health-wise is just not there," says Dr. Walter C. Willett, chairman of the department of nutrition at the

Harvard School of Public Health. "Often the organic is fresher and tastier, but it's not the most critical factor from a health standpoint. The important thing is to make sure you're getting the fruits and vegetables."

Still, if you're worried about the chemical factor—but don't like the high prices—you might want to choose to go organic in those products that tend to use more pesticides.

"For myself, when I think about those issues for my family, I try to identify products that tend to have heavy pesticide residues," says Dr. Meir J. Stampfer of the Harvard School of Public Health. "For instance, strawberries have high pesticide residues, so I try to get organic."

In 2006 the Environmental Working Group (www.ewg.org), a nonprofit environmental watchdog organization in Washington, D.C., compiled the "dirty dozen," a list of fruits and vegetables containing the highest levels of pesticides. They are peaches, apples, bell peppers, celery, nectarines, strawberries, cherries, pears, imported grapes, spinach, lettuce, and potatoes. Those containing the lowest pesticide levels are onions, avocados, frozen sweet corn, pineapples, mangos, asparagus, frozen peas, kiwis, bananas, cabbage, broccoli, and papayas.

Even so, experts say, don't let the pesticide issue scare you away from eating fresh produce. "The benefits of fruits and vegetables far outweigh any potential risk that pesticides might have," says Elizabeth Somer.

Tip: Thoroughly rinse fresh produce before eating (and don't use soap because it can leave a film). ☡

{be a nutrition sleuth}

Before buying any product, experts say, read the fine print on the Nutrition Facts label and the ingredients list, which are required by the FDA. Be cautious about advertising claims made on the package; terms like "all natural" or "fat free" can be misleading (fat-free products can be loaded with sugar and calories, for example).

"Food companies are out to sell products; most

of them are not always looking out for your health," says Elizabeth Somer.

"These days calories dominate any discussion of nutrition," says Marion Nestle, author of *What to Eat.* "I always look at calories first, then portion size because labels can be tricky. A 20-ounce soda label says it has 100 calories, but that's per 8 ounces. Drink the whole thing and you will have to walk three miles to work off those calories. As for processed foods, I recommend those that have fewer than five ingredients and don't contain any words you can't pronounce."

When reading the ingredients list, remember that items are listed from largest to smallest amounts. Here are some things to watch for:

Additional sugars. If the first ingredient is sugar and the second is high-fructose corn syrup, that's a bad sign. "You don't want sugar in the first three ingredients and you don't want sugar listed under numerous names throughout the list," says Somer. Added sugars can masquerade under other names: corn syrup, brown sugar, molasses, honey, concentrated apple juice or grape juice, dextrose, fructose, glucose, sucrose, or maltose (the suffix *ose* is a clue).

Trans fats. If you see words like "hydrogenated" or "partially hydrogenated" oils, the product contains artery-clogging trans fats. Put the package back on the shelf. ⬡

{10 rules for preserving nutrients}

Fresh fruits and vegetables are superstars, loaded with vitamins, minerals, and fiber. But after harvesting, it can take many days before they arrive in stores. The more time they are in transit and storage and exposed to the elements, the more their nutrients are compromised. To maximize the health factor when you buy produce, follow these rules:

1. Choose produce in bright and deep colors: berries, citrus, melons, red peppers, tomatoes, sweet potatoes, dark leafy greens, broccoli, and so on; the more colorful the produce, the greater the amount of antioxidants.

2. Eat fresh produce within a few days of purchase—the less time stored, the better.

3. Don't buy huge amounts—only what you will consume in a few days.

4. Store most produce in plastic bags in the refrigerator at about 32°F (exceptions: mushrooms—refrigerate but put in paper bags rather than plastic; tomatoes—they can lose flavor with refrigeration; bananas—they will turn black when refrigerated; and potatoes and onions—store them in a cool, dark place).

5. Store fruits and vegetables in separate bins—many fruits (apples, for one) emit ethylene gas, which accelerates decay in vegetables.

6. Remove any moldy or damaged pieces (mold can spread to other fruits and vegetables).

7. For safety, wash all fresh vegetables and fruits (even the precut and prewashed varieties) before eating them. But don't wash, cut, or chop them until you are ready to eat them.

8. When possible, try to eat the peels and skins, which generally are rich in nutrients.

9. When cooking, use light, quick methods like stir-frying or steaming in a small amount of water; high temperatures (boiling or deep-frying) will reduce vitamin C levels.

10. When fresh isn't an option, buy frozen produce, which is usually packed in ice as soon as it is picked; cold inhibits the enzymes that destroy nutrients. Canned fruits and vegetables also can be healthful (though they may lose some nutrients during processing), but make sure they don't contain additives such as sugar or sodium. ☑

Sources: Adapted from materials from the United States Department of Agriculture and the Food and Drug Administration

{your size guide}

Do you know what 3 ounces of meat looks like? How big 1/2 cup of mashed potatoes or pasta is . . . 1 1/2 ounces of cheese . . . a serving of juice? To guesstimate the amount on your plate, get familiar with these visual clues for serving sizes:

Food Group	One Serving Is About the Size of . . .
Grains Group	1 slice bread, 1 pancake, or 1 waffle = stack of 3 computer diskettes
	1 cup dry cereal = baseball
	½ cup cooked pasta or rice = small computer mouse or deck of cards
	1 bagel = hockey puck
	1 tortilla = 7-inch plate
	4 small cookies (vanilla wafers) = 4 casino chips
Vegetable Group	1 cup raw leafy vegetables = baseball
	½ cup cooked vegetables = small computer mouse or deck of cards
	10 french fries = small computer mouse or deck of cards
	1 small potato = small computer mouse or deck of cards
Fruit Group	½ cup sliced fruit = small computer mouse or deck of cards
	1 medium fruit = baseball
	¾ cup juice = 6-ounce can
	¼ cup raisins = large egg

Milk Group	8-ounce glass of milk = small (8-ounce) milk carton
	8-ounce container of yogurt = baseball
	2 ounces of cheese (mozzarella sticks) = 2 Magic Markers
	1 ½ ounces hard cheese (cheddar) = two 9-volt batteries or a C battery
Meat and Beans Group	2 to 3 ounces meat, poultry, or fish = small computer mouse or deck of cards
	2 tablespoons peanut butter = roll of film or Ping-Pong ball
	½ cup beans = small computer mouse or deck of cards

Source: The American Dietetic Association's Complete Food and Nutrition Guide *by Roberta Larson Duyff. Reprinted with permission of John Wiley & Sons, Inc.*

Perchance to Dream: A Good Night's Sleep

Sleep is the best meditation.

—HIS HOLINESS THE DALAI LAMA

Sleep is as fundamental as breathing and eating, but it isn't easy to get these days. In this 24/7 world, finding dream time can be a challenge when you're trying to juggle the responsibilities of work, family, and running a household. But, experts say, to function at our best and for overall good health, most adults need seven to nine hours of sleep every night. The essentials for optimum snoozing are:

A relaxed state of mind

A dark, cool, quiet room

A stimulant-free body at least three to six hours before bedtime

A reasonably early dinner, avoiding heavy or spicy meals at least three hours before bedtime

Daily exercise but nothing strenuous at least three to
four hours before bedtime

A comfortable mattress and pillow and clean bedding

A regular waking and sleeping schedule

The Land of Nod

It's a fact: We are a tired nation. Though all of us toss and
turn from time to time, for many people getting a sound
sleep is as elusive as a cloud. A 2003 study by the National Institutes of Health estimated that about 70 million Americans
have sleep-related problems. And women are more inclined
than men to have difficulties, particularly insomnia—
defined as the inability to fall asleep or to stay asleep—and
to experience daytime sleepiness (if you work a night shift,
you're particularly at risk), according to the National Sleep
Foundation.

Why? Blame it on the complexities of biology, sociology,
and plain old everyday stress.

First, there's the hormonal factor: Over the course of a
woman's lifetime, fluctuating levels of estrogen and proges-
terone have a crucial impact on sleep.

"It begins with a girl starting her menstrual cycle, then
you get into pregnancy and lactation, perimenopause and

menopause, and for a good fifty years we're floating around with hormones that are affecting sleep," says Dr. Joyce A. Walsleben, coauthor of *A Woman's Guide to Sleep* and research associate professsor of medicine at New York University Sleep Disorders Center.

Then there's the role women play in society. "Life gets in the way," Dr. Walsleben adds. "And for women that cannot be a factor that's ignored, because no matter how good men are, women are the primary caregivers. But it's not only your children, it's your aging parents and everybody else in the family who thinks mothers should know. So that always factors into how women sleep."

And when you throw in the pressures of holding a job, commuting, financial worries, and maintaining a home, it adds up to a lot of stress. For many women, the mental noise of the day can be hard to tune out when they lie down, Dr. Walsleben says. "Most women like to ruminate, to think things over and take them to bed, and that also gets in the way of sleep."

Men also have their share of sleep problems. "They are more prone to sleep apnea than women," says Dr. Walsleben. With sleep apnea, the breath becomes obstructed because airways are blocked; breathing actually stops. The most common signs are loud snoring and daytime sleepiness. Left undiagnosed, sleep apnea can be very serious; it puts men at risk for heart attack, stroke, high blood pressure, and diabetes, among other things.

Who is at risk? "The older men are, the more likely they are to have it," Dr. Walsleben says. "Men may develop sleep apnea in their thirties and forties, and they can certainly develop it as kids." Being overweight is another factor. When men are overweight, they tend to have "a big belly," which affects breathing.

Sleep apnea can be helped by wearing a masklike device called a CPAP (continuous positive airway pressure), which keeps the airways open.

Another sleep problem that men have more than women, Dr. Walsleben says, is REM behavior disorder. In this condition, dreams are acted out during REM (rapid eye movement) sleep, the stage of sleep when we dream. The condition can often erupt in violent behavior. "Men will swing their arms, fight, or scream," Dr. Walsleben observes. "They will say, 'I was driving and I fell off the road,' or 'I was having a fight,' and they'll smack their wife while they're asleep."

Older men are more likely to be affected; the disorder generally starts up when men are in their sixties. It is treated with medication.

Why We Need a Good Night's Sleep

Sleep is a basic human need, yet it is still something of a mystery to researchers. What is sleep?

"We don't know the answer," says Dr. Meir H. Kryger, author of *A Woman's Guide to Sleep Disorders* and director of Research and Education, Gaylord Sleep Medicine, Wallingford, Connecticut. "In other words, sleep is a state of being. We know it's important because in experiments, if you deprive animals of sleep, they will die. So there is something about sleep that is vital to being alive."

As to why we need adequate sleep, the most commonly accepted theory is that it has a restorative, healing effect on the mind and body, affecting, among other things, memory and learning, the immune system, and the nervous system.

Experts say that when we don't get the sleep we need, we can amass a kind of sleep debt that can eventually have serious psychological and physical consequences, taking a toll on daily functioning and overall health.

"There is evidence that sleep plays a key role in memory consolidation and stabilizing cognitive functions—attention and memory in particular," says Dr. David F. Dinges, chief of the division of sleep and chronobiology in the University of Pennsylvania department of psychiatry and associate director of the Center for Sleep and Respiratory Neurobiology at the University of Pennsylvania School of Medicine. "The cognitive effects relate to a whole host of things—from learning in school to driving safely to making corporate decisions to knowing what to do in an emergency. There is virtually no aspect of human behavior that attention and memory don't relate to in some profound way."

The ripple effect of inadequate sleep can be devastating, especially when it comes to auto safety. Fatigue is the cause of more than 100,000 accidents a year, resulting in 40,000 injuries and 1,550 deaths, according to the National Highway Traffic Safety Administration.

And there are other risks.

"The literature right now is not conclusive by any means, but it's very suggestive that a reduction in sleep doesn't just make you tired and cognitively impaired, it may have links to many other abnormalities," Dr. Kryger says. For example, chronic lack of sleep can impair the immune system. "A study published in the *Journal of the American Medical Association* showed that when sleep-deprived people were immunized for influenza, the vaccine did not work as well," he says. "Another study recently reported that people who sleep too much or too little have an increased death rate from cardiovascular disease."

Some research also suggests a link between inadequate

sleep and obesity, depression, mood disorders, high blood pressure, stroke, and diseases like diabetes.

Getting What You Need

First, there is no magic number when it comes to sleep needs. "It's like asking what the ideal shoe size is—it varies from person to person," says Dr. Kryger. "For most people the number is between seven and nine hours. But there are some people who do well with six and there are some people who need ten."

The amount you need depends on your circadian rhythms, an internal clock in your brain that regulates sleep and wakefulness over a twenty-four-hour period. Affected by the natural cycles of darkness and sunlight, body temperature, and the hormone melatonin, this clock monitors when we are active and when we are sleepy. Our body temperature fluctuates throughout the day, according to the cycle of our clock. When we are exposed to darkness, we become drowsy and there is an increase in melatonin, causing body temperature to drop; when we are exposed to light, we become more alert and there is a decrease in melatonin, causing body temperature to rise. So when our body temperature is low, we tend to be the sleepiest, which is generally early dawn, late afternoon, and bedtime; and when it is high, we are most alert, usually late morning, early afternoon, and early evening.

Of course each person's clock is different, which accounts for the reason why some of us are night owls and some of us are larks and some of us fall somewhere in between. Owls have slower clocks and tend to wake up and go to bed later, while larks have faster clocks and tend to wake up and go to bed earlier. To determine your sleep needs, you need to identify where you fall in the spectrum.

How do you know if you're getting enough sleep? "When you wake up in the morning and feel awake and alert and you don't feel the need to have a stimulant like coffee," Dr. Kryger says. On the other hand, he says, "If you're not getting what you need, you'll be tired."

Here's another clue. "If you find yourself nodding off in the afternoon at meetings or falling asleep in theaters, then either you're not getting enough sleep or you're not getting good-quality sleep. And the two go hand in hand," Dr. Walsleben says.

Sleep is affected by a combination of physical, mental, and environmental factors.

While most people experience a restless night now and then, it's important to point out that chronic insomnia is a symptom, so it's crucial to see a doctor. Troubled sleep can be associated with underlying medical conditions like thyroid imbalance, diabetes, allergies, heart irregularities, depression, anxiety problems, or sleep disorders such as apnea, narcolepsy, and restless legs syndrome. Also, certain medications—such as antidepressants, antiepileptics, blood pressure drugs, diet pills, and even over-the-counter anti-histamines, nasal decongestants, and diuretics—can disrupt sleep, so if you already have insomnia issues, be sure to find out the side effects before taking any drug.

Essentials: What the Experts Say

If you're a healthy person, experts say you can improve your chances of getting a good night's sleep by incorporating these basics:

A relaxed state of mind. To sleep well, you must learn to let go of the cares of the day. "Allow yourself to get sleepy," says Dr. Dinges. "Allow yourself to engage the processes in the brain that take it offline from the outside world and let it drift away."

To help yourself drift away, it's important to have a daily winding-down ritual. "You cannot run around all day like a chicken with its head cut off and expect to then turn it off at bedtime," says Michael Krugman, author of *The Insomnia Solution* and founder of the Sounder Sleep System, a self-healing method of promoting sleep. "It's important to have some kind of technique to use during waking hours to make your life more peaceful. When your life is more peaceful, your sleep is more peaceful."

Before turning in, do things that lower your stress level—whether it's meditation, prayer, progressive relaxation exercises, light reading, taking a hot bath, massage, deep breathing, drinking a cup of soothing herbal tea, listening to relaxing music, or having sex. Avoid activities that may upset you or stimulate you (excluding sex, which is a good thing).

"Don't argue at night, don't balance your checkbook, and don't go on the Internet," says Dr. Kryger. Experts say your bedroom should be a haven, a place reserved only for sleep and sex—keep your television in another room (TV can be stimulating, and you don't want that). If you have a lot on your mind, write it down in a journal or make a list before going to bed—when you've slept well, things really do have a way of looking better in the morning.

*A **dark, cool, quiet room**.* The environment where you sleep should be completely restful. Too much light, extremes in temperature, or unnecessary noise can be disruptive.

First, keep your bedroom as dark as possible. Darkness and light have a profound effect on us, telling us when to sleep and when to wake up. All human beings have circadian rhythms, internal body clocks that regulate sleep and wakefulness. This clock (the suprachiasmatic nucleus), located in the hypothalamus area of the brain, operates on an approximately twenty-four-hour cycle. Experts say looking at bright lights before or during sleep can disrupt the cycle. "Light can shift the circadian timing of our sleep," says Amy R. Wolfson, Ph.D., author of *The Woman's Book of Sleep: A Complete Resource Guide,* and a professor of psychology at the College of the Holy Cross in Worcester, Massachusetts. "If a light is left on or even a television is left on, it can enter the visual track and make you think you are ready to wake up before it's time to wake up. Even if you use a night light or a digital alarm clock, position them so they are not visible from your bed."

On the other hand, light has alerting effects and resets our clock each morning, so be sure to get daily exposure to light, especially during the dark winter months. "The sleep-wake cycle is a fundamental biological rhythm that is regulated by sunlight," says Michael Krugman. "And if we don't have sunlight to tell us when the day starts, then the body gets out of sync and sleep gets confused."

A cool room is preferable at bedtime. Keep in mind that your body temperature drops as you sleep. While there is no ideal temperature for sleeping, some researchers say 62 to 65 degrees is probably a good ballpark figure. Of course it's up to the individual, but try to avoid extremes. "It's a common-sense thing," says Dr. Walsleben. "If your room is 90 degrees, it can interfere with your sleep."

Your bedroom also should be quiet. Any kind of noise— a partner's snoring, street sounds, rambunctious neighbors, a squeaky ceiling fan, or the buzz of a loud air-conditioner— can affect the quality of your sleep. To counteract these types of disturbances, try using earplugs or a white noise machine.

A *stimulant-free body at least three to six hours before bedtime.* If you are prone to insomnia, stimulants like caffeine, nicotine, and alcohol can wreak havoc with your sleep. "Caffeine is a potent stimulant," says Dr. Dinges. "It takes three to seven hours for your body to metabolize it. There are studies that show that even the caffeine you drink in the morning can affect your sleep." Caffeine's effects can last ten to twelve hours in some people, according to the National Sleep Foundation.

"It's remarkable how long caffeine can stay in your system," Dr. Walsleben says. "If you're a female, you should not use caffeine after noon time if you have trouble sleeping. I don't even drink decaf in the afternoon. It can also interact with estrogen if you're taking supplements or birth control pills."

A word of caution for pregnant women: Caffeine can stay in the body hours longer because the caffeine metabolizes at a slower rate. Dr. Kryger recommends that if you're pregnant, limit yourself to only one cup of coffee a day. (For more on caffeine, see "Is Caffeine Hiding in Your Yogurt?" page 61.)

If you're a smoker and have trouble sleeping, it could be the nicotine that's keeping you awake. Nicotine, aside from the obvious risks it places to your health, is an even more powerful brain stimulant than caffeine, increasing heart rate and stress hormones. It also irritates the nasal passages and can exacerbate snoring. (An interesting note: Smokers are more likely to experience nightmares than nonsmokers, says the National Sleep Foundation.)

As far as alcohol, there's nothing wrong with a glass of wine with dinner, but don't overdo it. In other words, alcohol should never be used as an aid to sleep, experts say. "Alcohol is a depressant and as the body metabolizes it you are more likely to wake up," says Dr. Wolfson. Here's why: As the level of blood alcohol decreases, it sets in motion the sympathetic nervous system, which increases heart rate and signals the body to awaken. "People who are alcoholics tend to have a lot of difficulties maintaining sleep during the night," she says. "But even in terms of social drinking, if you have more than a small amount, it's going to interfere with sleep."

Alcohol also is dehydrating and can exacerbate snoring, so you're more apt to wake up. In addition, you will not have a satisfying sleep. Substances like alcohol and many drugs suppress rapid eye movement sleep (known as REM), which is the stage of sleep when we do most of our dreaming (see "Z's: The Basics," page 59). Many sleep researchers believe that dreaming is an essential component of emotional and mental health. "Some research suggests learning and memory consolidation takes place during REM sleep," Dr. Wolfson says.

"You might say, 'But I have alcohol or coffee or whatever with dinner, and I don't seem to have any problems,' " Dr. Wolfson comments. "What I often say is, 'Well, you are lucky, but if we studied you in a sleep lab your sleep might look different from someone who didn't use those substances.' What happens is your sleep becomes very inefficient and of poor quality."

A reasonably early dinner, avoiding heavy or spicy meals at least three hours before bedtime. At night, as our body goes into sleep mode, our biological systems, including digestion, slow down. Eating too much before bedtime, particularly hard-to-digest fats and proteins, puts a strain on our digestive systems. The result? Indigestion, gas, or heartburn. "As the body attempts to metabolize the food, and if it's difficult to do so, you will wake up and you may have difficulty falling back to sleep," Dr. Wolfson says.

Remember that food gives us energy, raising our metabolism and body temperature—not what you want before bed. Of course this doesn't mean you should go to bed hungry. "The old saying 'Don't go to bed stuffed or starved' may not be a bad rule of thumb," she says. A light snack—a banana or whole-grain crackers—is fine, experts say. But be careful what you eat, because some foods can induce or inhibit sleep. Complex carbohydrates, for example, are sleep-inducing because they produce a calming effect by increasing serotonin, a neurotransmitter that slows down the brain; on the other hand, proteins are sleep inhibitors because they produce alerting effects by blocking serotonin. Other sleep inhibitors: sugary foods and refined carbohydrates, which raise blood sugar levels, revving up our energy levels. (For more information on food, see "The Stuff of Life: Nutritious Food," page 5.)

Daily exercise, but nothing strenuous at least three to four hours before bedtime. Regular exercise can be a boon for sleep because it not only relieves stress but it also raises our body temperature. About four hours after rigorous activity, our body temperature drops significantly, which helps us fall asleep and stay asleep. But the time of day you exercise can affect your sleep. Since rigorous movement raises body temperature, it has alerting effects, so if it's done too close to bedtime, it can delay your sleep. "Exercise produces arousal and we need time for that arousal to subside," says Michael Krugman. So, experts say, try to do rigorous exercise—say, training for a marathon—either during the day or late in the afternoon. But, Krugman cautions, even some "benign" exercises can be tricky. For example, some yoga positions can be stimulating if done too close to bedtime. "It's important to know that backbends are highly excitatory, so if you do a vigorous round of them in the evening, it's going to affect your sleep." On the other hand, he says, "Forward bends are inhibitory, they tend to produce relaxation." (For more information, see "The Right Moves: Regular Exercise," page 65.)

A comfortable mattress and pillow and clean bedding. Since we spend about a third of our lives in bed, it makes sense to make it as sleep-friendly as possible. A lumpy mattress or a deflated pillow can cause discomfort and any number of aches and pains. Mattresses, box springs, and pillows should be replaced periodically, not only because they lose their flexibility and support, but they—as well as your bedding (sheets, pillowcases, and mattress pad)—can also be a breeding ground for dust mites, a major obstacle to a good night's sleep if you have allergies. Experts say you should change your mattress and box spring every five to seven years (some experts say up to ten years) and change your pillow more frequently (depending on the quality of the material). And change your bedding once a week (twice a week if you perspire a lot).

Is there an ideal mattress? No, experts say. Whether soft or firm, "it's your comfort that matters," says Dr. Walsleben, who also is a consultant for the mattress company Serta. But going softer might be a better choice for certain people, says Dr. Kryger. "One of the things I've discovered with my own patients is that if they have a painful condition, say, arthritis or pain in hips or knees, they seem to do better on a bed that's softer." The comfort rule also applies to pillows; look for one that supports your head and neck and keeps your spine straight. (For more on how to buy linens, bedding, and mattresses, see "A Roof over Your Head: Shelter and Safety," page 179.)

A regular waking and sleeping schedule. Experts say you should wake up and go to bed at the same time every day, even on weekends and holidays. By keeping a consistent schedule, your body gets the signal that it's ready for sleep. "Going to bed and waking up within about an hour of the same time is what's recommended, and when you start to deviate from that, you throw off the timing of your circadian rhythms," says Dr. Wolfson. Random or inconsistent sleep-wake times confuse your circadian rhythms, or internal body clock—particularly body temperature—making it more difficult for you to get to sleep and stay asleep.

Problems commonly arise when people try to catch up on lost sleep over the weekend. "Although you are getting more sleep or possibly making up for the lost sleep you got during the week, you shift your schedule," Dr. Wolfson says. The result can be Sunday-night insomnia and Monday-morning blues. Remember that when we are exposed to sunlight, we become more alert and our body temperature rises. By sleeping later, you delay these rhythms. So when you try to sleep on Sunday night, your body temperature will be high and you may have trouble getting to sleep.

{z's: the basics}

Sleep is not a luxury; it is a necessity for our health and well-being. In fact, we're hardwired for it. All human beings have an internal biological clock—called circadian rhythms—which regulate sleep and wakefulness. This clock, located in the hypothalamus in the brain, operates on an approximately twenty-four-hour cycle. It is affected by external light and dark, body temperature, and the hormone melatonin (which our bodies produce when we get drowsy).

Each person's clock is different, of course, which is why some of us are night owls and some of us are larks (late-to-bed owls have slower clocks, while early-to-bed larks have faster clocks). According to where we are in the cycle, we tend to feel sleepy at particular times—for example, early dawn, late afternoon, and bedtime—and more alert in the morning, early afternoon, and early evening.

In the last decades researchers have learned more about what happens in the brain while we sleep.

There are five stages that recur in each cycle, which last 90 to 110 minutes:

Stage one. This is a short drowsy period between sleep and wakefulness when our muscles, eye movement, and brain waves begin to slow down. During our waking hours when the brain is most active, it produces high-frequency electrical signals called beta waves. As we become drowsy, beta waves slow down, becoming alpha waves. As we get more relaxed, alpha waves turn into even slower theta waves.

Stage two. This is a period of light sleep, believed to be the start of true sleep, when our body temperature begins to drop and our heart rate decreases. Our muscles become more relaxed, and we begin to become less aware of the world around us. During this stage, theta waves combine with beta waves, producing short bursts of electrical activity called sleep spindles.

Stages three and four. These are the periods of deepest sleep, when there is no eye movement or muscle activity. Our brains begin producing much slower delta waves. During these stages, it is difficult to be roused from sleep.

Stage five. This is the REM (rapid eye movement) sleep period. This stage is different from the other four: Our brain becomes more active, our eyes move rapidly, and our heart rate and blood pressure rise. We do most of our dreaming during this stage.

Researchers say that we usually will repeat this five-stage cycle four or five times during an eight-hour sleep.

Source: National Institute of Neurological Disorders and Stroke

{is caffeine hiding in your yogurt?}

If you find yourself tossing and turning, caffeine could be the culprit. While the stimulant is a well-known component in coffee and tea (an 8-ounce cup of coffee has about 88 to 160 milligrams of caffeine; an 8-ounce cup of black tea has about 40 milligrams of caffeine, and green tea has about 20 milligrams of caffeine), it is also found in many common foods, soft drinks, and over-the-counter medications. Here are some common caffeine sources:

Excedrin (2 tablets, 130 mg)

Red Bull (80 mg)

Diet Coke (45 mg)

Mountain Dew (55 mg)

Sunkist Orange Soda (41 mg)

Ben & Jerry's Coffee Almond Fudge Frozen Yogurt (1 cup, 70 mg)

Dannon Coffee Yogurt (6 ounces, 36 mg)

Hershey's Special Dark Chocolate Bar (1.45 ounces, 31 mg) (Note: the darker the chocolate, the higher the caffeine; a milk chocolate bar contains about 6 mg.) ⬀

Source: Energyfiend.com and Center for Science in the Public Interest

{to nap or not to nap?}

For healthy people, taking a nap can be a great way to recharge when you're feeling drowsy. But the time of day and duration of the nap are key factors. "Naps can be very restorative and we know for sure that they have a positive effect on learning and memory acquisition," says Michael Krugman, author of *The Insomnia Solution*. "As long as they're not too long or too late in the day." Taking a siesta that's too long or too close to bedtime can interfere with night-time sleep, so it's best to nap during the day, preferably early afternoon. Experts say don't nap after four P.M.

A general rule of thumb: Keep the nap short, anywhere from fifteen to forty-five minutes but no more, experts say. "Anything beyond that will tend to make you groggier than when you started because you will start going into the deeper stages of sleep," says Dr. Meir H. Kryger, author of *A Woman's Guide to Sleep Disorders*. While naps can refresh you, they are not a substitute for adequate nighttime sleep. "Napping is a way of supplementing your sleep," says Dr. David Dinges, chief of the division of sleep and chronobiology of the University of Pennsylvania. "It helps but it's a little like living on fast food. It's not a substitute for a good diet, for getting an adequate night's sleep." Note: If you have insomnia, napping is not advised. 🖸·

The Right Moves: Regular Exercise

Lack of activity destroys the good condition of every human being, while movement and methodical physical exercise save it and preserve it.

—PLATO

It's no secret that regular exercise is essential for good health. For decades, study after study has extolled the benefits of an active life. But for many of us the word *exercise* conjures images of boot camp drudgery, pulled hamstrings, and a lot of huffing and puffing. But the old "no pain, no gain" days are long over. The buzz words now are "gain without pain." Experts say exercise does not have to be strenuous or time-consuming to be beneficial for overall health. Activities done at moderate intensity—brisk walking, for instance, for as little as thirty minutes on most days of the week—offer substantial health rewards. The point is to get moving. In 2007 the American College of Sports Medicine and the American Heart Association revised their physical activity guidelines for heathly adults under age sixty-five and those age sixty-five and over. The essential exercise components for good health are:

Cardio exercise (under age sixty-five): moderate intensity for thirty minutes a day, five days a week, or vigorous intensity for twenty minutes a day, three days a week; (sixty-five and over): moderate aerobic exercise for thirty minutes a day, five days a week, or vigorous aerobic for twenty minutes a day, three days a week.

Strength training (under age sixty-five): eight to ten exercises, eight to twelve repetitions each, twice a week; (sixty-five and over): eight to ten exercises, ten to fifteen repetitions each, two to three times a week.

Flexibility exercise: regularly (especially for those sixty-five and over).

Bodies *Not* in Motion

By now, with so much media attention given to the importance of exercise, it would seem that a lot more people would be lolling on the couch a lot less. But that's not necessarily the case—at least at the moment. First, the positive news: the most recent study from the Centers for Disease Control and Prevention reports a rise in the number of Americans who are engaging in regular physical activity—an 8.6 percent increase among women and a 3.5 percent increase among men. Now, the reality check: while those numbers are reassuring and show much progress, the fact is that more than half the population still do not get the recommended amount of regular exercise they need.

Inactivity—coupled with a diet high in calories—shows in our expanding girth. According to the Centers for Disease Control and Prevention, 66.3 percent of Americans are overweight or obese—putting millions at risk for all kinds of health problems, particularly diabetes and heart disease. The CDC reports that between 1976 to 1980 and 2003 to 2004, obesity among adults aged twenty to seventy-four rose from 15.0 percent to 32 percent.

A sedentary life was not a part of nature's plan. "It's ingrained in us genetically and physiologically to move," says Dr. Lisa Callahan, author of *The Fitness Factor* and medical director of the Women's Sports Medicine Center at the Hospital for Special Surgery in New York. (She also is director of player care for the New York Knicks and New York Liberty.) "If you look at us as evolutionary creatures, we were not designed to sit around."

In the past, physical activity was a natural part of life and work. The majority of Americans toiled on farms or had labor-intensive jobs, had fewer household conveniences (no self-cleaning appliances in those days), and didn't have automobiles. Today many of us are desk jockeys with sedentary office jobs; we sit for hours in front of the television or computer in our leisure time, drive instead of walk, have houses full of labor-saving devices, and often eat fast food or refined foods high in calories.

The problem for most of us today is time. We work long hours, we have families to care for, we're tired, and we can't seem to fit in exercise. But experts say that even a minimum of thirty minutes a day can reap rewards; the trick, they say, is to make fitness a daily habit, like bathing or flossing your teeth.

Why We Need Regular Exercise

There are so many benefits to exercise—it's not a hard sell. Among other things, it lowers the risk for heart disease, diabetes, high blood pressure, osteoporosis, and even certain cancers, particularly colon and breast cancer. Exercise also improves sleep, controls weight, and eases swelling from arthritis. And it is beneficial for the mind and spirit: It elevates mood and sharpens thinking, reduces depression and anxiety, promotes relaxation, and even improves your sex life.

As an added bonus, exercise will give you a better quality of life as you age.

The latter is very critical, experts say, because we are living longer. Studies show that maintaining an active lifestyle can help counteract the physical decline associated with aging. "We know the inevitable aspects of the aging process on all the systems of the body, from the muscles, bones, and joints to the heart and lungs and everything else, and one of the key ways to keep those things in shape is exercise," says Dr. Marilyn Moffat, coauthor of *Age-Defying Fitness* and a professor of physical therapy at New York University.

Dr. Moffat says we can help prevent or slow down many types of age-related deterioration. In her book she has identified what she calls the "five domains of fitness"—posture, strength, flexibility, balance, and endurance—areas of the body that decline most as we get older. She says we should concentrate on building up and improving these areas over our lifetime. And we should start while we're young. Some deterioration can begin even in the spring of youth. For instance, our posture can start changing as early as our teen years, says Dr. Moffat, caused by "prolonged sitting, using a computer, and carrying a heavy purse or briefcase."

So the more fit we are, the more independent we will be and the less medical care we will need in our later years.

"The idea is that when you get to the end of your life, you're still reasonably healthy, that you don't have these long and drawn-out periods where you're ill and frail and the end of your life is just miserable," says Dr. Janet Fulton, an epidemiologist and fitness specialist at the Division of Nutrition and Physical Activity at the Centers for Disease Control and Prevention in Atlanta.

Essentials: What the Experts Say

Experts say a good exercise program should include these components:

Cardio exercise. *What it is:* Any sustained activity—like walking, running, cycling, swimming, climbing stairs, and jumping rope—that increases your heart rate and maintains it over a period of time. Cardio should be the central focus of any exercise plan. *What it does:* Increases blood flow and oxygen; improves functioning of the brain, heart, lungs, and circulation; burns calories and fat; builds endurance; and controls weight. *What you need to do:* The updated guidelines from the American Heart Association and the American College of Sports Medicine say that to maintain good health, adults under sixty-five need moderate-intensity cardio activity at least thirty minutes a day, five days a week, or vigorous cardio at least twenty minutes a day, three days a week; adults sixty-five and over need moderate aerobic exercise for thirty minutes a day, five days a week, or vigorous aerobic exercise for twenty minutes a day, three days a week. To lose weight and maintain it, adults may need sixty to ninety minutes of exercise. *Note:* You don't have to do the thirty or sixty minutes all at once; you can break up workout time into ten- to fifteen-minute increments.

The beauty about many cardio exercises is that you don't need equipment and you can incorporate them easily into your lifestyle. Walking is one of the safest ways to start, but there are many activities you can consider. "Jumping rope is an intense conditioning activity you can do with very minimal equipment and almost no space," says Dr. Moffat.

What is moderate intensity? "If you're walking, it means moving briskly enough to get your heart rate up and to be breathing a little hard," says Dr. Callahan of the Hospital for Special Surgery in New York.

But, says Dr. Fulton of the CDC, "You don't want to be so out of breath that you can't say your name." Breaking a little sweat is fine but not necessary. "If health is your goal, moderate exercise, what I call no sweat, is more than sufficient," says Dr. Harvey B. Simon, author of *The No Sweat Exercise Plan: Lose Weight, Get Healthy, and Live Longer,* editor in chief

of the *Harvard Men's Health Watch,* and an associate professor of medicine at Harvard Medical School. The goal is to
get moving—any way you can. Dr. Simon says all kinds of
physical activity can be beneficial—even household chores
like raking leaves, sweeping, cleaning, gardening, mowing
the lawn, or washing the car.

If you're in good health and you want to do a more intense workout, consider interval training, a fast-slow program that alternates between short bouts of high-intensity
cardio exercise—such as running, biking, swimming—and
short periods of moderate, low-intensity activities.

Strength training. *What it is:* The use of resistance in the
form of free weights, machines (like Nautilus, Cybex, or
Universal), or elastic bands to build strength in the major
muscles of the upper and lower body. *What it does:* Increases
muscle endurance and strengthens bones as we age, increases overall strength, reduces the risk of fractures and
the development of osteoporosis in later years, helps with
balance and mobility, and may ease arthritis pain. *Added benefit:* A recent study suggests that lifting weights just twice
a week may help reduce abdominal fat. *What you need to
do:* (under age sixty-five) eight to ten exercises, eight to
twelve repetitions each, twice a week; (sixty-five and over)

eight to ten exercises, ten to fifteen repetitions each, two or three times a week. (*Tip*: Don't exercise the same muscle groups on consecutive days.) *Note:* Some floor exercises—such as sit-ups, push-ups, and squats—also will help build strength.

Some women shy away from strength training because they fear their muscles will start to ripple like the Incredible Hulk. Not to worry, experts say. "A normal female with normal hormones will never take on the muscular definition of a male regardless of how much work she does, unless she injects herself with testosterone," says Dr. Walter R. Thompson, a fellow of the American College of Sports Medicine, coauthor of the *ACSM Fitness Book,* and professor of kinesiology and health at Georgia State University in Atlanta.

To get the most out of strength training and to avoid injury, it's important to do it properly (get some professional instruction if you can). Some key areas to focus on are:

• *Form*. This is your technique. Movements should be slow and controlled when you lift and lower the weight—about two to four seconds each way. Never swing the weight or sway on your feet—if you do, the weight probably is too heavy for you.

• *Range of motion.* This is the full extension of the muscle being worked. For example, if you are doing bicep curls, begin by extending your arm at your sides and slowly lifting the weight to the shoulder—don't start midway with the elbow bent. "If you go through an incomplete range of motion, you're not getting the maximum benefit of the exercise," says Dr. Callahan.

• *Amount of weight.* The idea is to fatigue the muscle by lifting the maximum amount you can lift. The weight should be challenging but not so heavy that it's uncomfortable. As you gain strength, you will find the weight easier to lift, so gradually increase it in small increments to make it a little harder. "If your idea of strength training is lifting five-pound dumbbells for the rest of your life, you're not going to make much progress," says Dr. Callahan.

Flexibility exercise. *What it is:* Stretching major muscle groups. *What it does:* Lengthens and loosens the muscles, reduces the risk of injury, improves posture, range of motion, mobility, balance, and coordination, promotes relaxation, and improves overall performance. *What you need to do:* Stretching exercises can be done daily or several times a week as part of your regular workout program. *Complementary exercises:* Techniques like yoga, Pilates, and tai chi are excellent for flexibility and balance and also help keep core muscles strong.

Flexibility is one area of fitness that tends to take a back seat, but it is extremely important. When muscles are tight and inflexible, the chance for injuries like pulls, strains, and so on is increased. Also, as we age, our muscles lose suppleness, which can affect our sense of balance and coordination, putting us at risk for fractures from falls. "Aerobic conditioning and strength training have traditionally been stressed in the exercise-fitness arena, and yet from my perspective, posture, balance, and flexibility should be equally important especially in light of the fact that we're all living longer and longer," says Dr. Moffat of New York University.

Men especially need to loosen up. "They are a lot less flexible than women, and it does contribute to injuries," says Dr. Simon of the *Harvard Men's Health Watch*. "They really need to do flexibility exercises, especially as they get older. But look around, who goes to yoga? It's women."

To get the most from stretching:

• Do a warm-up before stretching (see below) to get the blood flowing to your muscles.

• Don't bounce when holding a stretch (you can tear the muscle)—the movement should be controlled and slow.

• Hold the stretch position for about 30 to 60 seconds.

• Stretch before and after your workout.

Other considerations. *Balance training.* Dr. Moffat says we can improve our balance by doing specific exercises such as one-legged stands (standing on one leg and holding the position for thirty seconds), head turns (side to side, chin up and down), and tandem walking (placing one foot in front of the other).

Importance of warm-ups. A warm-up generally is any aerobic/cardio activity done in a very brief spurt that gets your heart rate elevated and the blood flowing. Muscles need to be warmed up before doing any exercise. "If you go from doing nothing to all-out exertion very quickly, number one, you're likely to get hurt. Number two, it's just uncomfortable. And number three, it puts a big stress on your heart," says Dr. Callahan. "Warming up means just easing into an activity gradually." But stretching is not a warm-up, she says. You should warm up cold muscles even before you stretch. "Muscles generally respond better to stretching once they're warm," she says.

Experts say a warm-up could be anything from jumping jacks to jogging—but done at a lower level. "Let's say you want to run a seven-minute mile," Dr. Callahan says. "It's not the smartest idea to go out the door, especially in the cold, and start running that mile. Start by walking or jogging to get your muscles warmed up a bit and then pick up the pace."

Getting Off on the Right Foot

Now that you know what you need, you're just itching to jog around the block, right? Well, don't—at least not right this minute. To reap the rewards of exercise and to stick with it, you must—and this is important—*must* find a fitness plan that works for you as an individual. If you don't, the simple fact is you will likely get discouraged and give up. (Exercise, like dieting, has a high dropout rate.)

"I don't think it's appropriate anymore to come out with a single set of guidelines that we can apply to everybody," says Dr. Simon. "One size doesn't fit all. People in different age groups and health groups have different needs for things like strength, stretching, and balance."

To create a good program, experts say you need to assess the following areas:

Your goals. What do you want to accomplish? Are you exercising to improve your health or to lose weight? For instance, if weight loss is your goal, you'll need to exercise more than thirty minutes a day for five days a week to burn calories.

Your physical condition and age. Your fitness level and age will determine the kind of exercise you need. Have you been sedentary a long time? Are you overweight? Are you over fifty? Do you smoke? Do you have any medical problems? If so, it's advisable to get a medical checkup and a fitness evaluation before starting any exercise program. To assess your health risks, two measurements are helpful: body mass index (BMI), which calculates the percentage of body fat through weight divided by height (a BMI of 30 or more is considered obese), and waist-to-hip ratio, which is waist size divided by hip size (apple shapes carry excess weight around the abdomen and are at greater risk for heart disease and diabetes than pear shapes, who carry weight around the hips, buttocks, and thighs).

Your exercise preferences. What do you like to do? Do you prefer exercising alone or with others? Finding enjoyable activities—whether it's snowboarding or Bavarian folk dancing—is the key to a successful exercise program. "I never say the best exercise is walking or jogging or whatever," says Dr. Thompson. "The best exercise is what motivates you to get out there every day."

Your lifestyle. How much time do you have? How can you best fit exercise into your day? Can you exercise during your lunch hour? How convenient is it for you—can you do it at home or at a local park, or would you rather join a gym or health club? Are there facilities within walking distance of your home or job, or do you have to drive there? (Convenience is a major consideration, especially during the winter months, when the urge to hibernate sets in.)

Learning to Stick with It

Those of us who belong to gyms or health clubs see it every year: Come January there's a huge surge of new members who, buoyed by New Year's resolutions, are determined to get into shape or lose a few pounds. But it's always the same outcome. Within a few months, the crowds begin to recede, and by March it's pretty much back to the regular gym rats.

"The statistics on exercise program adherence are abysmal," says Dr. Thompson. "Study after study has demonstrated that within three to six months over half the people that start programs drop out."

Why? The most common reasons are injuries, taking on too much at once, discouragement or boredom, unclear goals, or just plain lack of knowledge. "What often happens is that people either overdo it or underdo it," says Dr. Simon of Harvard. "They hurt themselves, or they find it too difficult, and quit, or they underdo it and they think that's enough. That's why I've tried to establish that one size does not fit all."

Exercise should not be a rigid plan—it should be simple and tailored according to your needs. "One of the reasons people say they don't like to exercise or that they're intimidated by exercise is because we've made it more complicated than it has to be," says Dr. Callahan. "If you get the basics down, you can mix it up in a lot of different ways."

Here are some tips to make your life more exercise-friendly:

Start slowly. If you've been sedentary, taking on too much at once is a surefire way to get discouraged or, worse, injured. Keep it simple at first. A great way to begin is by walking. "Walking is a good way to start because it's easy, you know how to do it, and you don't need equipment, other than comfortable shoes and clothes," says Dr. Callahan. Walking is also one of the safest exercises you can do. As Thomas Jefferson once said, "The sovereign invigorator of the body is exercise, and of all the exercises walking is the best."

Set attainable goals. One of the reasons we get discouraged with exercise is that we don't set realistic goals for ourselves. "What people fail to do is develop short-term and long-term goals," says Dr. Thompson. For example, if you're exercising to lose weight, begin with small goals. "Many people will say, 'I'm going to lose twenty-five pounds by Christmas,' and that becomes their goal. But that's a long-term goal. A short-term goal is, 'I'm going to lose a pound and a half or two pounds this week and another two pounds next week.' If you set up short-term attainable goals, you will have lost the twenty-five pounds by Christmas."

Get an exercise buddy. For many people, having someone to work out with can be a great motivator—whether it's a friend or as part of a group in a classroom environment. "You do not need to join a gym, but social support is one of the big indicators of being physically active and continuing it," says Dr. Fulton of the CDC. "There's a whole area of study about how to get people to be more active, and the one thing that always comes up is having someone to do it with. Social support always helps."

Do activities you like. This is really the key to success—boredom is the death knell for any exercise program. Dr. Callahan says that whenever her patients say they don't like to exercise, she tells them, "You just haven't met the one that you like yet." If you love the outdoors, then try to do things like hiking or skiing. On the other hand, if yoga is the only thing you like to do, that's fine, too. "I'm a big believer in tailoring things that make sense for my patients," she says. "If a woman loves yoga, then I would support her but ask her to try to get in a couple of fifteen-minute walks a day to add to the cardio benefit."

Consider hiring a personal trainer. A personal trainer is not a necessity, but you may want to consider it even if it's just a one-time arrangement. Here's why: A good trainer will review your fitness goals with you and show you how to optimize your workout time. He or she will instruct you on how to use strength-training equipment and how to do proper stretching and warm-up exercises.

The challenge is finding someone who's top-notch. Just because a trainer works at a gym or health club, don't assume they're qualified to teach you. "The problem is that the health and fitness industry is totally unregulated," says Dr. Thompson. "My suggestion would be to seek out guidance from someone who has both the educational background and certification from a legitimate certifying agency like the American College of Sports Medicine, the National Strength and Conditioning Association, or the American Council on Exercise."

{get moving—any way you can}

Exercise doesn't have to be a structured program in a gym. Experts say you can increase your activity level by incorporating small changes into your daily life. Here are a few of their suggestions:

• When doing local errands, try walking or cycling instead of driving.

• If you have to drive, park your car a few blocks from your destination and walk the rest of the way.

• If you commute by bus or train, get off a few stops early and walk.

• Climb the stairs instead of taking the elevator or escalator.

• Carry your groceries to the car instead of using a shopping cart.

• When watching TV, don't use the remote control—get up and change the channels manually.

- Take a walk after lunch or dinner.

- Ask a friend to exercise with you or enroll in a class.

- Do mat exercises like squats, crunches, and push-ups while watching TV.

- Choose fun activities like skating, biking, or dancing.

- Wash and wax your car by hand. ☑

{pregnancy and exercise}

Should you exercise during pregnancy? A resounding yes, says the American College of Obstetricians and Gynecologists (www.acog.org). ACOG says that at least thirty minutes of exercise on most days of the week can help ease a lot of the woes that pregnancy brings—backaches, constipation, and bloating and swelling, among other things. Walking, swimming, cycling, and strength training are excellent choices, but you should take these precautions:

- Avoid activities with jumping, jarring motions, or quick changes in direction that may strain joints or cause injury.

- Avoid downhill skiing, racquet sports, contact sports, and scuba diving.

- Take care not to get overheated, especially in hot, humid weather—as it can lead to fluid loss and dehydration.

- Drink plenty of water to avoid overheating.

- Exercise within reason, not to the point where you're exhausted.

- After the first trimester, avoid doing any exercises on your back.

- Wear comfortable clothing that will keep you cool.

- Wear a well-fitting bra that supports and protects your breasts. ☑

Source: Adapted from Patient Education Pamphlet No. AP119 © 2003 American College of Obstetricians and Gynecologists

{no more sprains, strains, or pulled tendons}

One of the major reasons why people stop exercising is that they get injured. In fact, Americans (especially aging baby boomers) seek medical care for musculoskeletal injuries more than any other type of injury. Why? Some of us are weekend warriors who overdo it; some of us are just not as young as we used to be. Whatever the reason, you don't want to be a health statistic. Here are some ways to avoid trauma:

• Listen to your body. If an exercise doesn't feel right or you experience pain, stop immediately.

• If you've been sedentary for a while and are just starting out, go slowly. Things tend to go wrong when we overdo it.

• Allow recovery time of at least a day between strength training sessions—never work the same muscle groups on consecutive days.

• Always warm up and stretch before working out. Cold tight muscles leave you vulnerable to injury.

• Wear good-quality shoes with cushioned insoles and good arch support, and wear lace-up shoes instead of slip-ons—they offer much more support. Make sure the shoes are the right choice for whatever activity you're doing and that they fit properly, with a wide enough toe box to accommodate your foot. Women especially should think comfort and support—not fashion. "Most women's sneakers are made with a more narrow toe box because it makes the foot look better, so I often suggest that women with wider feet think about buying boys' or men's sneakers," says Dr. Marilyn Moffat, a professor of physical therapy at New York University. Replace your shoes every three to six months, depending on how much weight-bearing activity you do. "When shoes are worn out, the probability of you becoming injured is a lot higher," says Dr. Janet Fulton, an epidemiologist in the Division of Nutrition and Physical Activity at the CDC.

• Protect your knees. A knee injury can have a

devastating effect on mobility. To keep the joint flexible, strengthen the leg muscles that support it, especially the quadriceps. Also, wear good-quality shoes and lose any excess weight—when we walk, the pressure on each leg is double our body weight, and when we run or climb stairs, the pressure quadruples, adding even more stress to the joints. Women should take special care to protect their knees, because they are at higher risk than men for injuries involving the anterior cruciate ligament, or ACL (the elastic tissue at the front of the knee that controls twisting motions). This may have to do in part with biology: women have looser ligaments than men, and their wider pelvic shape creates a larger angle between the hips and knees, putting more stress on the knee joint.

• Remember R.I.C.E. If you do get injured, the American Academy of Orthopedic Surgeons recommends the following guidelines for immediate treatment. R, for Rest: If you feel pain, stop all activity immediately. I, for Ice: Apply ice wrapped in a towel to the injured area. C, for Compression: To reduce swelling, wrap the ice pack on the area and apply pressure (but not so tight that it cuts off circulation). E, for Elevation: Raise the injured part to above heart level. ⬀

The Big Picture: Overall Wellness

The greatest wealth is health.

—VIRGIL

Wellness is more than just the physical. It is the whole picture: body, mind, and spirit. Wellness is about balance. Granted, there are factors we cannot change—our genetic makeup, for instance, which may increase our risks for certain illnesses or conditions. But DNA aside, we can lessen these risks and slow down the aging process through the choices we make: to eat right, to take time for ourselves, to develop close relationships, and to get adequate medical care. Ultimately, maintaining wellness is an investment in our future, because the way we live now will have a significant impact on our quality of life as we age. The essentials for wellness are:

Good lifestyle habits
Hopeful beliefs and attitudes
Connection with others
Preventive medical care
A safe environment
Self-care and self-nurturance

Why We Need Overall Wellness

If fifty is the new forty, then eighty is the new seventy. The good news is we are living longer today than ever before. According to the most recent figures from 2004, the average life expectancy in the United States is 80.4 years for women and 75.2 years for men. And more and more of us are living beyond that—the latest U.S. Census Bureau statistics show that 70,104 Americans are one hundred years or older, with women outnumbering men about four to one. As the first of the baby boomers soon begin reaching sixty-five, the number of centenarians is expected to reach more than a million by 2050. (To understand how far we've progressed, consider that in 1900 the average life span was forty-nine years for women and forty-seven years for men.)

These days we all expect to live a long and healthy life. And many of us will remain fit well into our later years. But some will show signs of early aging or succumb to disease and illness before their time. Why? The reasons vary—genes and environment do play a role. But, experts say, what largely dictates the state of our health—now and in the future—is in our own hands.

"The determinants of health are very different from what most people think they are," says Dr. John Swartzberg, chair of the editorial board for the *Berkeley Wellness Letter* at the University of California, Berkeley, School of Public Health. "We consistently hear about the big killers, like heart disease, stroke, cancer, diabetes, morbid obesity, and so on. But in reality the major determinants of health are the habits we have that are causing those things, and they are under our control to a large extent."

An Ounce of Prevention

Just about everyone on the planet knows the dangers of cigarette smoking, yet 21 percent of Americans are still puffing away. Unfortunately, according to the Centers for Disease Control and Prevention, smoking-related illnesses like lung cancer, heart disease, stroke, and emphysema claim the lives of more than 400,000 people each year. While breast cancer is the most common cancer in women, and prostate cancer the most common cancer in men, lung cancer is actually the leading cancer killer of both women and men.

The CDC reports that since 1950 lung cancer deaths among women have increased 600 percent (not all smoking-related). The agency says that if you're a woman smoker, your life expectancy could be reduced by about fourteen years.

"Smoking is far and away the greatest cause of preventable serious illness. It's a no-brainer," says Dr. Andrew Weil, author of many bestselling books, including *Healthy Aging* and *Eating Well for Optimum Health: The Essential Guide to Food, Diet, and Nutrition* and the founder and director of the Program in Integrative Medicine at the University of Arizona. "And because that habit starts quite young, I think that's where the focus has to be."

About 90 percent of adults who smoke cigarettes started the habit at or before the age of eighteen, according to the U.S. Department of Health and Human Services. Though smoking is on the wane among teenagers overall, some still haven't gotten the message. The American Lung Association says that 22 percent of high school students smoke (experts say a good many girls start because they think it will control their weight).

Drinking is another risky behavior that starts young, usually in adolescence. The average age for girls to try alcohol is thirteen and for boys it is eleven. Teens begin to drink regularly by age 15.9, reports the National Clearinghouse for Alcohol and Drug Abuse. More than three million teens are estimated to suffer from alcoholism and several million have drinking problems. For teens as well as adults, the effects on health can be devastating. Among other risks, alcohol impairs judgment, increasing the chance of accidents, injury, and violence as well as the likelihood of engaging in behaviors like unsafe sex and smoking. It is linked to depression, liver disease, heart disease, hypertension, osteoporosis, birth defects and other complications during pregnancy, and certain cancers (some research suggests that even moderate use of alcohol can increase the risk of breast cancer).

But prevention is not always uppermost in people's minds, especially when they're young. Heart disease, for example, is the number-one killer of both women and men—but the damage may not be apparent until years later. "Heart disease is highly preventable, but people just don't want to think about it," says Dr. Alice D. Domar, the author of *Self-Nurture: Learning to Care for Yourself As Effectively As You Care for Everyone Else*, the executive director of the Domar Center for Mind-Body Health in Waltham, Massachusetts, and an assistant professor of obstetrics, gynecology, and reproductive biology at Harvard Medical School. "They think, 'If I have a cheeseburger every day when I'm twenty and have a heart attack at seventy, so what?' We just don't want to think about prevention."

Yet about 17.4 percent of American teens between twelve and nineteen years old are overweight, according to 2004 figures from the National Institute of Diabetes and Digestive and Kidney Diseases. Children and teens who are overweight are at high risk for developing serious illnesses like heart disease and type 2 diabetes—conditions that were once thought of as adult illnesses but are now being found in young people.

The point is that living longer will not mean living better if we don't maintain health in our younger years. The focus, says Dr. Domar, should be on "keeping young people healthy so they don't become sick elderly people."

While it's not possible yet to reverse the aging process, it is possible to slow it down by preventing the diseases and conditions that can compromise the quality of our lives. Of course that doesn't mean you have to live your life in a bubble. It's all a matter of balance.

Essentials: What the Experts Say

Do you want to maintain wellness throughout your life? Here's what you need:

1. Good lifestyle habits. Developing positive behaviors is one of the best ways to ensure good health. The way to do that is to:

- Eat a wide variety of nutritious foods, with emphasis on fresh vegetables and fruits, whole grains, lean protein, and healthy fats. Avoid processed and refined food, trans fats, and excess salt and sugar.

  Women of childbearing age need adequate amounts of iron and folic acid. Good nutrition is essential for a healthy pregnancy. "I like women to start thinking about their diets in their teenage years—that their body is a garden and that they're getting it well fertilized for the time a seed gets planted," says Dr. Christiane Northrup, the author of many bestselling books, including *The Wisdom of Menopause: Creating Physical and Emotional Health and Healing During the Change* and *Women's Bodies, Women's Wisdom: Creating Physical and Emotional Health and Healing*. (For more on what to eat, see "The Stuff of Life: Nutritious Food," page 5.)

- Exercise regularly, at least thirty minutes a day, five days a week. Physical activity strengthens the heart muscle and bones, lowering the risk of cardiovascular disease and osteoporosis respectively. It also reduces stress and lowers the risk of diabetes, high blood pressure, and even certain cancers. (For more on exercise, see "The Right Moves: Regular Exercise," page 65.)

• Get adequate sleep, at least seven to nine hours (or the amount you need). According to the National Sleep Foundation, sleep deprivation increases the risk for, among other things, motor vehicle accidents, obesity (lack of sleep is believed to affect the chemicals and hormones that control appetite), diabetes, cardiovascular problems, and depression and substance abuse. It also lowers our attention span, reaction time, and ability to learn. (For more on sleep, see "Perchance to Dream: A Good Night's Sleep," page 41.)

• Maintain a healthy weight. Being overweight or obese will put you at risk for heart disease, diabetes, hypertension, certain cancers, and other diseases—and some research suggests that your life expectancy could decline by five years. More bad news: The overweight and obesity rates among adults in the United States have more than doubled over the last thirty years—and the number has more than tripled among children and teens.

• Practice ways of minimizing stress. One of the downsides of modern life is that many of us are over-extended, juggling the responsibilities of family and relationships, home, work, finances, and so on. How you respond to these daily pressures is crucial. Some of us live in a state of constant worry, and the cumulative effect of this stress can take its toll. Stress has been linked with insomnia, depression and anxiety, obesity, digestive problems, heart disease, and other illnesses. "I don't think we can live without stress, but we can learn ways to minimize its harmful effects," says Dr. Weil.

To decrease stress, engage in activities that promote relaxation: meditation, prayer, deep breathing, yoga, tai chi, massage, or whatever works for you. (For more on the benefits of meditation and prayer, see "Mind Fitness: Physical and Mental Exercise," page 301; and "Still Water: Time for Reflection," page 337.)

• Don't smoke—it is one of the worst things you can do to your body. It will increase your risk for developing cardiovascular disease, stroke, and certain cancers, specifically of the lung, throat, cervix, esophagus, bladder, and mouth. It may also increase the likelihood of early menopause, weaken your bones, stain your teeth, give you bad breath—and, as an added bonus, age your skin and give you wrinkles (not to mention the negative effects on pregnancy—among them premature birth and low-birth-weight risk). There's nothing good to say about smoking.

• Don't drink alcohol to excess. Like some of life's pleasures, drinking has an upside and a downside. While it may be heart-healthy in small amounts, it also has the potential for abuse. Too much of it can have a severely negative effect on health. The watchword: if you drink, do it in moderation. That means about one glass a day for women and two for men. "Alcohol has some health benefits, especially red wine," says Dr. Weil. "But there are also many minuses. The key is moderation. And for women moderation is less than it is for men because the role of alcohol as a factor in breast cancer seems very clear. So women who have a family history of female blood relatives with breast cancer should be especially cautious about alcohol."

• Limit exposure to ultraviolet radiation by avoiding direct sunlight at midday (ten A.M. to four P.M.) and avoid tanning beds and sunlamps. Overexposure to UV rays will put you at risk for skin cancer and premature wrinkling and aging of the skin (however, we do need about fifteen minutes a day of sun for the production of vitamin D). According to the American Cancer Society, skin cancer is on the rise among people under forty years old. Use a sunblock (with zinc oxide or titanium dioxide) or a sunscreen with at least a 15 SPF (sunblocks generally provide greater protection than sunscreens), wear broad-brimmed hats, long-sleeved shirts, long pants (dark colors are more protective), and UV-protective sunglasses. And avoid indoor tanning facilities. A recent study found that people who used tanning beds in their teens and twenties had a much higher risk for developing squamous cell carcinoma and the more deadly melanoma.

• Practice safe sex if you are not in a trusting, monogamous relationship. That means always using a condom. Physical intimacy is one of life's greatest pleasures, but if you don't use protection, you are putting yourself at risk for any number of dangerous diseases, including herpes, gonorrhea, syphilis, chlamydia, human papillomavirus (HPV), hepatitis, and the HIV virus.

2. Hopeful beliefs and attitudes. The power of the mind cannot be underestimated when it comes to wellness and health. An increasing number of studies suggest that having an optimistic outlook—the inherent belief that life is good, that it has purpose and meaning, and that things will work out for the best—may strengthen the immune system and increase longevity.

"I think good health starts with the way you think," says Dr. Northrup. "I think it's overlooked but it's the most important thing. There were studies done by Dr. Becca Levy at Yale that tracked people's beliefs about their health. My favorite one was about people's attitudes about aging. They found that people who had a sense of optimism about getting older lived on average seven and a half years longer than those who had a negative belief."

Dr. Northrup says that people who have positive beliefs also tend to cultivate positive behaviors. "When you value yourself, then you value your health and you naturally want to do the things that enhance it. Addictions, smoking, overeating, and so on—people don't do those things unless they're trying to make themselves feel better about some thought or belief that they're not worth anything. That's why people reach for the drink or the doughnut they don't need. It's their belief system. If you work on that, then the diet is simple."

Having a strong belief system also helps us cope better with life's stresses and adversities, she says. "There will be times when things will happen—you're going to get sick, for instance," says Dr. Northrup. "So it's important to have a belief system that includes room for being human, room for compassion for yourself, room for seeing illness as a reset button in your body—not as punishment for having done something wrong. We have a long history in Western civilization of somehow beating ourselves up if something bad happens—that somehow we were wrong or bad. And so you need a way to think about life's crises that gives them meaning for yourself, where you're not feeling like a victim. You need some kind of spiritual belief system that there's a meaning here that's bigger than we are." (For more on optimism and belief systems, see "Surviving the Slings and Arrows: A Sense of Control," page 257.)

3. Connection with others. We are all social beings and need love, affection, companionship, and sexual intimacy. Having close relationships—a loving partner as well as supportive friends and family—gives our lives meaning. It gives us a sense of belonging. Research suggests that people who feel isolated and alone have shorter life spans and suffer from more health problems than those who have strong social bonds (a CDC report says married people live about five years longer than single or widowed people). Feelings of loneliness and isolation are major contributors to stress, anxiety, depression, alcoholism, and drug abuse.

"Certainly one of the essential ingredients to health is having a social fabric—friends, family, coworkers, people you have strong nurturing connections with," says Judy Norsigian, executive director and coauthor of *Our Bodies, Ourselves* and cofounder of the Boston Women's Health Book Collective. "You support them and also feel supported—it's mutually reinforcing. It doesn't have to be one big network, but you have to have at least one and several is better. That way you don't experience the many health problems that come with isolation."

Some research has shown that people with fewer social contacts have lower immunity. "They've done studies on immunity and social support at the University of Pittsburgh where they took cold virus and sprayed it into people's noses and throats," says Dr. Northrup. "And they found that those people who had four or more different social groups were the least likely to get colds." Another study, at Carnegie

Mellon University, found that among first-year college students who received flu shots, the students who felt lonely had a poorer immune response than those who had larger social networks.

We all need social ties, but in the midst of our hectic lives, friendships can take a backseat. "If you look at the data from the last ten years on the power of social support, it's profound," says Dr. Domar. "But research shows that when a woman is busy she continues to meet the needs of her job, her home, and her family, but she lets go of her friends. A woman cannot let go of her friends. She needs someone or a group of someones to confide in."

On the whole, though, women are more likely than men to have a wider circle of support. Close friendships are something that men need, too, but these relationships are not always a priority, especially when men are married. "Women have more social ties than men," says Dr. Harvey B. Simon, editor in chief of the *Harvard Men's Health Watch*, author of *The No Sweat Exercise Plan: Lose Weight, Get Healthy and Live Longer*, and associate professor of medicine at Harvard Medical School. "Most married men depend on their wives for a majority of their social networks outside of work. Everything runs through the wife, whereas women tend to have social networks and friendships apart from their spouses."

Having social ties is a crucial part of maintaining overall health and wellness, Dr. Simon says. "People are good medicine, and I think that this is one of the multiple factors accounting for the fact that women live 5.2 years longer than men."

For more on connection, see "Reaching Out: Love and Connection," page 249; and "In Harmony: A Sense of Oneness and Connection," page 321.

4. Preventive medical care. Getting preventive screenings and immunizations as well as regular checkups are important elements in maintaining wellness (for women this also includes doing monthly breast self-exams beginning at age twenty).

For instance, it is crucial to detect cancer in the early stages, when it is easier to treat, and routine screenings like mammograms and colonoscopies can save lives. While there has been some controversy about the effectiveness of mammograms, the National Cancer Institute says they detect 80 percent of abnormalities and reduce breast cancer deaths in women ages forty to sixty-nine. Women in high-risk groups should also get MRIs.

Colonoscopies are another effective tool in prevention. Colon cancer is the second leading cause of cancer death in men and women. "We can probably prevent most of it through colonoscopies, yet only about 40 percent of people who should be getting them are getting them, from the latest numbers I've read," says Dr. Swartzberg.

Dr. Simon recommends that men in their sixties who were or still are smokers should get an ultrasound to test for abdominal aortic aneurysm, which is a weakening of the aortic wall. Men, he says, are much more prone to this type of aneurysm than women.

Immunization can be another weapon in thwarting certain illnesses. According to the CDC, each year at least 45,000 American adults die from the flu, pneumonia, and hepatitis B—and about 200,000 Americans are hospitalized just from the flu alone. (There are vaccines that prevent these illnesses; see "What You Need: Immunizations for Adults," page 117). There has been much debate about vaccines, particularly with regard to children. "There are questions about immunization, such as are we giving too many vaccines or are we giving them too early," says Dr. Weil. "But I think the basic idea of them is good and I think the benefits outweigh the risks." If you have any concerns about risks, always consult your doctor first before getting any vaccine.

One way to make sure you are getting the proper screenings and immunizations for your age group—and to maintain wellness—is to have regular checkups with your primary care provider. The National Institutes of Health recommends that you have at least two physical exams during your twenties; after that, up to age sixty-five, have a checkup every one to five years, and after age sixty-five, have one every year.

Dr. Swartzberg says it's important to see your doctor regularly for a variety of reasons. "I wear my hat as a practicing internist, as well as a teacher, and I like the idea of getting together with my patients just to catch up with them to see how they're doing, to talk about any lifestyle issues they have, and to make sure that the newer things we can offer patients are available to them."

Also, keep current medical records. "I think it's very important to keep a file of your medical information, including family history, past illnesses, and results of physicals and blood tests," says Dr. Weil.

One more prevention tip: Don't neglect teeth, skin, eyes, and ears. Here are the current recommendations from the U.S. Department of Health and Human Services:

- *Teeth:* All age groups should have a dental checkup once or twice every year. It is very important to brush and floss every day—good dental hygiene not only prevents cavities, gum disease, and bad breath; it also may inhibit serious illnesses. Studies show that people with dental problems such as gingivitis and periodontitis may be at greater risk for developing cardiovascular problems. Why? Scientists aren't certain, but one possible theory is that harmful bacteria in the mouth get into the bloodstream through inflamed gums and then travel to the heart and other organs of the body.

• *Skin:* Have a skin exam every three years, beginning at age twenty. After forty, have an exam every year. All age groups should do a monthly self-exam for moles.

• *Eyes:* Have at least one eye exam from ages twenty to twenty-nine years old, and at least two exams from thirty to thirty-nine. After forty, have exams every two to four years, and at sixty-five and older, have an exam every one to two years.

• *Ears:* Have a hearing exam beginning at age eighteen, then every ten years until age forty-nine. After fifty, have an exam every three years.

5. A safe environment. We all need to feel safe, both for our health and our emotional well-being. That means living and working in a place where we are not exposed to hazards—air pollution (both indoor and outdoor), toxins in food, water, or other products, excess noise, and psychological abuse or physical violence. "You need to minimize toxic input to your body and your psyche, and that can be a lot of things," says Judy Norsigian, coauthor of *Our Bodies, Ourselves*. "It could be exposure to pesticides, air pollution, new construction that is emitting gaseous products or particulates from idling engines. But it could also be a person who's constantly intimidating or threatening you, someone you work with or someone you live with."

While some hazards may be difficult for us to control, we can take an active role in reducing others. For instance, smog and outdoor pollution are huge environmental problems, but the air we breathe in our homes (and at work) is actually a much greater threat to our health. The Environmental Protection Agency says that indoor contaminant levels can be two to five times—and sometimes more than one hundred times—as high as outdoor levels. Indoor pollution is so widespread that the agency considers it to be one of the top four environmental problems in the United States.

Indoor pollutants include biological contaminants like dust mites, mold, pollen, and animal dander; chemical contaminants like tobacco smoke, lead, radon, asbestos, and formaldehyde; and toxic substances in household cleaners, paints, and solvents. Exposure can cause eye, nose, and throat irritation, headaches, dizziness, nausea, fatigue, severe allergies, asthma or other respiratory conditions, and, in some cases, cancer. Some safeguards against indoor pollution: proper ventilation, air filters, not smoking, substituting safer products, and installing radon and carbon monoxide detectors.

Also, Judy Norsigian says, we can buy safer beauty and household products. "You can, with minimal effort, put fewer toxic things close to your body—from how you wash your clothes, to hair dyes and makeup, to cleaning products." For information about the safety of cosmetics, check the Environmental Working Group (www.ewg.org), an environmental watchdog organization that keeps a database of more than 23,000 brand-name products. Also check the National Library of Medicine (www.householdproducts .nlm.nih.gov), part of the National Institutes of Health. (For more on home safety, see "A Roof over Your Head: Shelter and Safety," page 179.)

If you want to reduce your exposure to pesticides, consider organic fruits and vegetables. They can be expensive, so you may want to go organic on those items that tend to be pesticide-heavy (check www.ewg.org for their list of "the dirty dozen"; also see "Organic Versus Conventional?" page 31).

There are additional measures we can take to protect our

health. "There's another whole dimension to this—it's avoiding potentially harmful practices and those that are known to be harmful," Norsigian says. For instance, women should avoid douching. "When you douche you're putting it right into your body. It has access to your bloodstream and your lymphatic system." The point, she says, "is to think twice before putting anything either on your body or in your body, before you take a drug or before you go through a surgical procedure that's elective in the hopes of looking more beautiful."

Another important aspect of being safe is to have nurturing relationships in our lives—both at home and at work. It is unacceptable to put up with any kind of violent or abusive behavior (this includes verbal or psychological harassment). According to estimates by the American Psychological Association, 4 million women a year suffer serious assault at the hands of domestic partners, and those numbers most likely are underreported. If you are living or working in a hostile environment, get help immediately. For domestic problems, contact the National Domestic Violence Hotline (www.ndvh.org or 800-799-SAFE), or the U.S. Department of Justice, Office on Violence Against Women (www.usdoj.gov/ovw or 202-307-6026). For work-related issues (including unsafe conditions), contact the U.S. Equal

Employment Opportunity Commission (www.eeoc.gov) or the National Institute for Occupational Safety and Health (www.cdc.gov/niosh/homepage.html). For more information on women and environmental health, check www.ourbodiesourselves.org.

6. Self-care and self-nurturance. An integral part of wellness is taking care of our own needs—whether it's our health care, our emotional life, or our spirituality.

Health care is one area where men especially fall short. The problem is that the majority of them delay seeking medical attention, or don't seek it at all—and that goes for physical illnesses as well as psychiatric problems. According to the Centers for Disease Control and Prevention, women are 100 percent more likely than men to visit the doctor for annual checkups and preventive services.

Neglecting health care has dire consequences. Men die at higher rates than women from the top ten causes of death, reports the Men's Health Network of the Department of Health and Human Services. They are also more likely to suffer from undiagnosed depression, which puts them at an increased risk of suicide. According to the Network, men with undiagnosed depression are four times more likely than women to take their own lives.

{screening and immunization chart}

WHAT YOU NEED: Screenings for Adults

Screenings	18–39	40–49	50–64	65 and older
Thyroid test (TSH) (Women)	Beginning at age 35, then every 5 years	Every 5 years	Every 5 years	Every 5 years
Blood pressure test	At least every 2 years	At least every 2 years	At least every 2 years	At least every 2 years
Cholesterol test	Beginning at age 20, then every 5 years	Every 5 years or consult physician.	Every 5 years or consult physician.	Every 5 years or consult physician.
Bone density test (Women)		Consult physician at onset of menopause if at risk.	Consult physician at onset of menopause if at risk.	At least once. Consult physician about repeated testing.
Diabetes	Consult physician if at risk.	Beginning at age 45, then every 3 years	Every 3 years	Every 3 years
Mammograms* (Women)	Consult physician if at risk.	Every 1–2 years Consult physician.	Every 1–2 years	Every 1–2 years
PAP test and pelvic exam (Women)	Every 1–3 years if you have been sexually active or are older than 21	Every 1–3 years	Every 1–3 years	Every 1–3 years

Screenings	18–39	40–49	50–64	65 and older
Chlamydia test	For women, yearly until age 25 if sexually active. Older than age 25, get this test if you have new or multiple partners. All pregnant women should have this test. Men should consult physician.	For women, get this test if you have new or multiple partners. All pregnant women should have this test. Men should consult physician.	Consult physician.	Consult physician.
Sexually transmitted disease (STD) tests	Both partners should get tested for STDs, including HIV, before initiating sexual intercourse.	Both partners should get tested for STDs, including HIV, before initiating sexual intercourse.	Both partners should get tested for STDs, including HIV, before initiating sexual intercourse.	Both partners should get tested for STDs, including HIV, before initiating sexual intercourse.
Fecal Occult Blood Test (FOBT)			Yearly	Yearly
Colonoscopy		Consult physician	Every 10 years if at risk.	Every 10 years
Sigmoidoscopy (with FOBT)			Every 5 years, if not having a colonoscopy	Every 5 years, if not having a colonoscopy

Screenings	18–39	40–49	50–64	65 and older
Double Contrast Barium Enema (DCBE)			Every 5–10 years, if not having a colonoscopy or sigmoidoscopy	Every 5–10 years, if not having a colonoscopy or sigmoidoscopy
Rectal exam	Consult physician.		Every 5–10 years with each screening (colonoscopy, sigmoidoscopy or DCBE)	Every 5–10 years with each screening (colonoscopy, sigmoidoscopy or DCBE)
Prostate-Specific Antigen (PSA) blood test (Men)		Consult physician.	Consult physician.	Consult physician.
Testicular exam (Men)	Monthly self-exam and part of general checkup	Monthly self-exam and part of general checkup	Monthly self-exam and part of general checkup	Monthly self-exam and part of general checkup

*The American Cancer Society recommends that women in high-risk groups also get annual MRIs; women should also do monthly breast self-exams beginning at age twenty.

Sources: Adapted from materials from the U.S. Department of Health and Human Services, Office on Women's Health; Centers for Disease Control and Prevention; and the National Cancer Institute.

WHAT YOU NEED: Immunizations for Adults

Immunizations	18–39	40–49	50–64	65 and older
Influenza vaccine (Flu)	Consult physician.	Consult physician.	Yearly	Yearly
Pneumococcal vaccine (Pneumonia)				One time only
Tetanus-diphtheria booster vaccine	Every 10 years	Every 10 years	Every 10 years	Every 10 years
Human papilloma-virus (HPV) vaccine (Women)	Recommended for ages 9–26, before becoming sexually active. Consult physician.			
Shingles vaccine			Age 60 and over, one time only	
Hepatitis A vaccine	One series for those in high-risk groups (lifestyle or occupation). Consult physician.			
Hepatitis B vaccine	One series for those in high-risk groups (lifestyle or occupation). Consult physician.			

Sources: Adapted from materials from the U.S. Department of Health and Human Services. Office on Women's Health; Centers for Disease Control and Prevention; and the National Cancer Institute.

Why are they so reluctant to seek help? "It's true, men don't like to take the time to take care of themselves," says Dr. Simon. "Nobody knows why this is so. Perhaps it's a cultural thing. Men adopt either the John Wayne, 'Grit your teeth and hope it goes away' macho approach or the ostrich 'Put your head in the sand and deny that anything is going wrong' syndrome. They don't like to admit that they're vulnerable. They don't even like to reveal themselves in conversation with their doctors. So they don't seek medical help often, and it's a grave mistake."

While women are more likely than men to seek medical attention, they tend to fall short on other areas of self-care and self-nurturance because they often put others' needs before their own.

"We have a health care model that says people should exercise and they should eat right and they shouldn't smoke and blah, blah, blah, but there's very little attention spent on how to get a woman to actually pay attention to her health, because her first priority is going to be the health of her family," says Dr. Domar. "We need to stop educating women about what they need to do for their health and start educating them to take care of themselves, their hearts and their souls. It's really hard for us to do that, and I think that's the crux in women's health."

Taking time for self can be a loaded issue for some women. "What I hear from women is that they love the concept of self-nurturance but they feel guilty every time they do anything for themselves," Dr. Domar says. "Guilt is probably the most troublesome emotion in women. They feel guilty over everything."

When women have families, they often put aside their own needs. "When you talk about preventing heart disease," she observes, "if a woman has the choice of serving her family broccoli and skinless chicken, something only she will eat, or serving cheeseburgers, which her husband and the kids will eat, what do you think she's going to do? She's not going to inflict her need for a low-fat diet on her family."

Because women are the nurturers of others, they often neglect nurturing themselves. "For a lot of women creativity often goes early," says Dr. Domar. "They are not feeling good about doing their watercolors if their kids are screaming. So they give it up."

But nurturers of others need to feed their own souls, too. "You cannot be doing and being and giving all the time," she says. "You have to have downtime. You need to meditate or crochet or draw or whatever. You need to be creative. You have to build into your life the things that bring you joy and happiness, and not make it just about changing diapers."

{red flags: women and heart attack}

Heart disease is the number-one killer of both women and men. While women account for nearly half of all heart attack deaths, there are differences in how women and men respond to attacks. Women are less likely than men to believe they're having a heart attack and more likely to delay seeking emergency treatment. In addition, they tend to be about ten years older than men when they have an attack. They also are more likely to have other conditions, like diabetes, high blood pressure, and congestive heart failure—which makes it all the more crucial that they get proper treatment fast. Here are the most common signs of a heart attack:

• Pain or discomfort in the center of the chest.

• Pain or discomfort in other areas of the upper body, including the arms, back, neck, jaw, and stomach.

• Shortness of breath, breaking out in a cold sweat, nausea, or lightheadedness.

Note: In both men and women the most common heart attack symptom is chest pain or discomfort. But women are somewhat more likely than men to experience shortness of breath, nausea/vomiting, and back or jaw pain.

If you feel these symptoms, call 911 immediately. ⬈

Source: The National Heart, Lung and Blood Institute. Adapted from material found at www.nhlbi.nih.gov

{a better life}

Our life expectancy has almost doubled since 1900. What accounts for this dramatic rise? The Centers for Disease Control and Prevention says it can be attributed to the many advances in public health over the last century:

• More availability of safer and healthier foods

• Better control of infectious diseases through clean water

• Vaccinations and sanitation

- Better access to neonatal and medical care

- Improved motor vehicle safety

- A decline in deaths from heart disease and stroke

- Increased awareness about the hazards of smoking

- Safer work conditions

Do you want to know how long you will live? To calculate your life expectancy, go to www.living to100.com. ⌕

{the best prevention, hands down}

Did you know that viruses can live for up to two days on surfaces like doorknobs, counters, or faucets? You can catch these germs by touching infected areas and then putting your hands to your eyes, mouth, or nose. The best way to avoid sickness is to wash your hands frequently with soap and warm water (fifteen to twenty seconds).

Here's how to reduce your close encounters with germs:

• Wash your hands *before* preparing food, eating meals, feeding your children, or touching your eyes, mouth, or nose, or treating a cut or wound.

• Wash your hands *after* preparing food (especially raw eggs, meat, or poultry), handling trash, blowing your nose, coughing or sneezing, using the bathroom, changing a diaper, touching someone who is sick, treating a cut or wound, or petting an animal or cleaning its waste.

• Avoid touching public playground equipment, public bus rails and armrests, shopping cart handles, chair and seat armrests, vending machine buttons, escalator handrails, public restroom surfaces, customer-shared pens, public telephones, and elevator buttons—these surfaces were found to be the grimiest in the United States by researchers at the University of Arizona.

• Regularly clean your telephone, cell phone, computer keyboard, and mouse—University of Arizona researchers also found these surfaces to be bacteria hotspots.

• Don't use anyone else's lipstick or makeup (and steer clear of testers in department stores).

• Throw away used tissues.

• Carry an alcohol-based hand sanitizer with you. ⬧

Sources: Centers for Disease Control and Prevention, American Society for Microbiology, American Dietetic Association, University of Arizona

On the Outside: Clothing

Fashion fades, only style remains the same.

—COCO CHANEL

Aside from its practical purpose—to give warmth and protection—clothing conveys a message to the world about who we are. Among other things, it can reflect our social and economic status, our personal taste, our self-confidence, and even our moods. Chosen well, it can maximize our assets and minimize our flaws.

Americans spend a lot on clothing—in 2006, $350 billion on apparel and footwear, according to the American Apparel and Footwear Association. But what portion of the "stuff" in our wardrobes do we actually wear? Not that much, apparently. Experts say the majority of people use only 20 percent of what's in their closet 80 percent of the time—

which means the rest of our clothes and shoes are collecting dust.

Is your closet bursting at the seams, yet you have "nothing to wear"? Insiders say the secret to dressing well lies in having a good foundation of timeless classics that work with everything, then building your fashion pieces around them. What are these classics? According to leading industry experts, the essentials for a woman's wardrobe are:

A black dress

Three skirts: black pencil; A-line; and (depending on body type) a pleated, dirndl, full, or boot-length

Two pairs of pants: slim and wide-leg

A pair of well-cut jeans

A classic white cotton shirt

A turtleneck

An assortment of camisoles, shells, tank tops, T-shirts

A cashmere sweater

A blazer

A jacket

A trench coat or lightweight coat

A winter coat (depending on climate)

The Well-Edited Wardrobe for Women

Contrary to what most people think, you don't need a lot of clothes to be well dressed. "The number-one key is having a well-edited closet," says Glenda Bailey, editor in chief of *Harper's Bazaar*. "Coco Chanel spent her life thinking about fashion, and when she died in 1971, she had only three outfits hanging in her Paris closet."

Having a well-edited closet means having clothes that make you look and feel your best and eliminating those that don't. This involves knowing what colors, shapes, and textures work best for your face and body type—and knowing how to put them all together in a very personal way. It's about finding your own style. Having style does not mean being a slave to fashion. Style is about knowing who you are and what suits you best—it's having the good sense to know that just because something is in fashion doesn't mean it's going to look good on you.

"Clothes are the props of our existence," says Bailey. "They should amplify our identity, not mask it. If you buy only pieces you love and pieces that say you, you can't go wrong."

But when it comes to buying clothes, a lot of us can go wrong. It's a good bet that on any given day many women look in their closets and say, "I've got nothing to wear." But the issue is not a lack of clothing. In fact, it's just the opposite, says Peter Walsh of TLC's *Clean Sweep*, author of *It's All Too Much: An Easy Plan for Living a Richer Life with Less Stuff.*

"People think that if they have more, they will have more

to select from, and if they have more to select from, some-how their choices will be easier," says Walsh. But it doesn't work that way, he says. "The fact is, you have to look at it differently. You have to ask yourself, 'What do I want from my clothes, and what do I want from my closet?' If the answer is, 'I want clothes that fit, that I look great in, that I'm complimented on. I don't want to be stressed when I walk into my closet in the morning, and I want to be able to find stuff easily and quickly,' then get rid of all the distracting clothes and cut it down to the core group that you wear, that fit you well, that you look good in, that you get complimented on."

Dana Buchman, the fashion designer, agrees. "You should just throw unflattering things out of your closet. You're much better off with a skimpier closet that has pieces that fit you beautifully. The whole point of fashion is to make you feel good, period. It's all about the feeling clothes give you."

"When your closet is well edited, it simplifies your life," says the fashion designer George Simonton, a professor of fashion design at New York's Fashion Institute of Technology and cohost of *I've Got Nothing to Wear* on TLC. "It's really a European mentality," says Simonton, who also appears regularly as a featured designer on QVC. "Europeans don't buy tons and tons like we do. They'll buy it and they'll wear it out."

What is your relationship with clothes? Are you a fashion victim, with racks of expensive "What was I thinking?" items? Are you a collector of "fat" and "skinny" clothes for wherever your weight happens to be on the scale? Are you a hoarder of ghosts from seasons past—still hanging on to Alexis Carrington dresses from high school, hoping they'll come back in style? Or are you a hunter-and-gatherer, with a closet full of sale and bargain items you just couldn't pass up but haven't worn—some with price tags on them years old?

Whatever it is for you, fashion experts say that having an unmanageable closet is not the road to successful dressing. If you want to create a wardrobe that works, keep it simple. Insiders say that you need a solid foundation of essentials. But that doesn't mean you shouldn't buy new trendy items, too.

"If you get basic pieces, then you can buy your fashion pieces around them," says the fashion designer Nicole Miller. "For instance, if you have an overstyled top and skirt, you can't wear them together. Even if they're from the same designer, it's unlikely that you would really want to wear an outfit that way. So if you are wearing a very over-the-top designer blouse, pick something low-key for the bottom."

Dana Buchman also says that you should build on essentials. Yet "you need fashion of the moment. You need to buy something new because it makes you feel good, it's modern, and it keeps you current. You need that new piece, that new color, that new shape or new category. It livens up your wardrobe and livens up your spirit. It's exciting to wear something new."

Women's Essentials: What the Experts Say

We all need a stable of versatile foundation pieces in our wardrobes, items that go with everything. Here, the pros offer their thoughts on the must-haves:

A black dress. "The little black dress—the Audrey dress—it's a classic," says George Simonton. While the black dress is a wardrobe basic, it should always be in a style that's fashionable, says Dana Buchman. In fact, it was not on her essentials list. "The reason I didn't put it on is that it works only if it's right for the moment—the dress I had seven years ago wouldn't work now. The little black dress has to be current."

Skirts.

The Pencil Skirt. Across the board, the black pencil skirt was the one constant on every expert's essentials list. "A slim black pencil skirt should graze the knee, not be too long or too short, and it should be in a top-quality fabric with beautiful feminine tailoring," says George Simonton. "It's got to have style," Dana Buchman adds. "Make sure it is pegged so it's tapered at the bottom." Jasmine H. Chang, executive editor of *O: The Oprah Magazine,* says a pencil skirt should make you "look long."

The A-Line Skirt. Glenda Bailey of *Harper's Bazaar* says the A-line is "universally flattering." Buchman says that for some women the A-line may be more slimming than the pencil skirt. "Women with fuller hips may prefer an A-line with some kind of movement."

Other Possibilities. Dressing well involves knowing your body type and what styles are most becoming on you. Nicole Miller thinks a pleated skirt in black or charcoal is a must-have, but it should be stitched down—fitted around the stomach so pleats don't open at the waist (that adds weight). Chang recommends a full or dirndl skirt that hits right at the knee. Simonton thinks a long, slim six-gore skirt (fitted around the stomach) is an essential. "A lot of women say they like the comfort of a longer, boot-length skirt," he says.

Pants. A great-fitting pair of pants are another must-have on every fashion expert's list. Most recommend both slim and wide-leg pants; it's a safe bet that one of them will be in style. "Every year there's a new pant shape—and sometimes there are two," says Dana Buchman. As far as color, black, of course, is classic; Jasmine H. Chang also recommends gray flannel.

One caution when buying pants, says Nicole Miller: If you want to look slimmer, "stay away from pleated pants and pants with details like pockets. Pleats and pockets make you look heavy. Buy flat-front pants, and you can wear all your fancy tops over them without any bulk under the blouse."

As an alternative, George Simonton suggests a good black pantsuit. You can wear it as a suit, or you can wear the jacket or pants separately, with other things in your wardrobe.

Jeans. Another universal essential. Chang says to get "a great pair of jeans that fit as well as they can." The key word is *fit,* says Buchman: "The fit is everything. They have to fit tight in the hip. They don't look good when the rise is too high and when they don't have any style."

*A **classic white cotton shirt**.* "This essential truly never goes out of style," says Jasmine H. Chang. "Jacket shoulders change, skirts get long and short, pants get low-waisted and high-waisted, skinny and full. Prints get boring when worn over and over again." Glenda Bailey and George Simonton are also fans of the white shirt.

But not everyone agrees on this one. Dana Buchman and Nicole Miller have reservations. White shirts, Buchman believes, "look great when you first put them on, but as soon as you ride in a car or get off the airplane or dry clean them a couple of times, they can get shabby-looking. To me, it's more important to have a piece of color." Says Miller: "Very few people look good in white shirts. You have to be superfashiony—you have to have the right belt and the right jewelry."

*A **turtleneck**.* This was another essential mentioned by most experts. The preferred color: black. Chang recommends merino wool, while Simonton likes cashmere. "A classic black turtleneck is fabulous," he says. "It's a great backdrop for a scarf or a pin."

*Tops **(underpinnings)**.* Another must-have on everyone's list: camisoles, shells, tanks, tube tops, or T-shirts, whatever you prefer. You can't have enough of them in your wardrobe. "You really need these layering pieces," says George Simonton.

"I hate to carry on about basic pieces," says Nicole Miller, "but you always need a basic black tank top to wear under a sweater—it could be a scoop neck or a jewel neck. I feel I need ten of those in my closet." Dana Buchman loves camisoles, but she isn't a big fan of the T-shirt. "Most T-shirts aren't pretty. You have to be careful with them—it depends on your age. As you get older, you have to be more particular about what you wear."

A cashmere sweater. Another all-time classic. "A cashmere cardigan goes with everything—it's universal," says Miller. "If you wear a dress, you can throw it on for the evening. Or you can wear it over a tank top or tubular jersey top." Buchman also loves the cashmere cardigan and says a pullover can work, too. "I have an oversize V-neck I always take with me to Paris, where I go every summer. I can throw it over my shoulders if I'm cold when taking a walk by the Seine. It's sensual to wear, sexy to the touch, and practical to travel with—it keeps me warm and it also makes a great pillow on the plane. Plus, it takes color beautifully." Simonton, also a fan of the cashmere sweater, recommends a twin set.

A blazer. Some experts think a blazer is more essential than a jacket; some think a jacket is more essential than a blazer. Some think they are equally essential. Simonton favors both. "You can't go wrong with a classic Ralph Lauren–type blazer. But make sure it's single-breasted because you might want to wear it open."

A jacket. "A great jacket is crucial—it doesn't have to be a blazer," says Dana Buchman. And the fit is everything. It should hang "beautifully from the shoulder—it has to fit you from the shoulder," she says. Simonton agrees that with jackets (as well as blazers and coats), tailoring counts: "It has to be good quality. You can tell if it's poor quality by the shoulder and the way the sleeve is sewn into the armhole."

A trench coat. Another classic that was on every expert's list. Trench coats "never go out of style, and they're very flattering," says Buchman.

A winter coat (depending on climate). "Everyone needs a good winter coat," says Nicole Miller. Because a coat is something you wear for probably more than one season, be sure it's tailored well, in a good-quality fabric, and in a style that will hold up. George Simonton recommends a wrap coat. "It's classic and flattering, and it doesn't go out of style."

Rules to Dress By, According to the Experts

Is your closet filled with too many odd and ends? Here, five leading fashion experts offer tips on how to create a wardrobe that works:

Dana Buchman:

1. Know your body shape and face shape. The only way to do that is to look in the mirror.

2. Don't wear anything you don't love, even if you bought it. It's never worth it.

3. Do purge your closet regularly; get rid of everything that you don't *love* to wear. (If you have an emotional attachment to something, because of emotional associations—good memories or whatever—then keep it in the attic, not in the "active" part of your closet. It will confuse you and slow you when you're looking for an outfit.

4. Never say never. I've met women who say, "I can't wear green." Well, there are four trillion shades of green. To block out a whole category leaves you limited. Many times I've been in dressing rooms where a woman will try on something and it will look fabulous and she'll say, "Oh, no." She's seeing something in her mind, something that's not in the mirror. You have to look in the mirror, not in the mirror of your mind.

5. Shop with a trusted friend—another pair of eyes can help lift you out of your old mind-set.

6. Have your clothes altered. A lot of women are lucky enough to buy off the rack, but most of us can't because we're all different combinations. It is essential to make things fit you beautifully.

Glenda Bailey:

1. Always apply the rule of three: Buy an item only if you can wear it with three other garments.

2. Three good skirts and three good pairs of pants are the building blocks for your wardrobe.

3. Have three tops for every bottom.

4. Don't wear more than three colors at once.

5. Consider your face shape—if you have a round face, avoid turtlenecks; if you have a long, thin face, polo necks are great; and V-necks look fabulous on everyone.

6. Before buying a piece, ask yourself if you are buying it for your real life or your fantasy life. I have a friend who works in fashion who spent thirty percent of her life at fashion shows and parties; fifty percent at the office; and twenty percent downtime with her kids. She had amazing clothes to wear out on the town, but nothing that didn't embarrass her children. Don't dress for a mythical life that you don't lead.

Nicole Miller:

1. Before you buy something, make sure that it goes with a lot of things. People often buy shoes because they love them, but they don't think about whether those shoes will go with anything. I can't tell you how many times I've bought shoes that go with only one thing.

2. Avoid buying pants with pleats and pockets—they can make you look heavy. Buy flat-front pants, and you can wear all your fancy tops over them and there won't be any bulk under the blouse.

3. When considering color, brown is as important as black. I feel I never have enough brown pieces in my wardrobe.

4. Be cautious with stripes. It's not so much whether the stripe is vertical or horizontal—it's the size of the stripe. Big stripes will always make you look heavier than thin stripes.

5. Stay away from patent leather. It always looks like plastic, no matter how expensive it is. Also, it's a trend that always goes out really fast.

George Simonton:

1. Buy clothes that are beautifully cut in a good-quality fabric and you'll never get lost.

2. Avoid clothes that are gimmicky—you know, those novelty things that make too much of a statement. Of course you don't want to get lost in the woodwork, but you don't want something that's so bold, that captures attention so much that people say, "Oh, she's wearing that electric-blue thing again." I want to see a woman's face. As I tell my students all the time, "You don't have to put bells and whistles on clothing."

Jasmine H. Chang:

1. Never invest in the "it" anything. What's the point of spending thousands of dollars on something that will be "so last season" in a few short months? Try bagborrowsteal.com instead.

2. Some people say it's a cop-out, but dressing black head to toe is still the best and most chic way to go. People never notice you're wearing the same pants for the third day in a row!

3. No tattoos, ever. Can people really commit to *anything* for their entire life?

4. Unmanicured feet will *kill* a hot pair of open-toe shoes or sandals. Consider a clean pedicure a fashion must-have accessory.

5. Some don'ts can look like do's. Experiment a little, you might be pleasantly surprised.

The Insiders: Their Top Choices

As you might expect, the fashion professionals interviewed did not agree on every essential. The master list of essentials earlier in this chapter was compiled from their personal lists. Here are their choices:

Glenda Bailey:

A black dress

A white shirt

A black pencil skirt

An A-line skirt (universally flattering)

A pair of slim pants

A pair of wide pants

A trench coat

A winter coat

A blazer

A jacket

T-shirts or camisoles

Nicole Miller:

A black dress

A cashmere cardigan

Tops: tanks, shells, tube tops, and T-shirts

A black pencil skirt

A black or charcoal stitched-down pleated skirt

A pair of black pants (side zip with a flat-front)

A lightweight coat

A good winter coat

Jasmine H. Chang:

A great pair of jeans that fit well

A pair of gray flannel pants

Classic white cotton shirts

A stylish lightweight coat or trench

A black merino wool turtleneck

A pencil skirt that makes you look long

A full skirt or dirndl that hits right at the knee

Dana Buchman:

The new pant silhouette of the season, in black

A great jacket

A pair of perfect-fitting jeans (stretch denim)

A sexy black pencil skirt (A-line if you have fuller hips)

Animal-print anything (never goes out of style)

A cashmere sweater

A turtleneck

Tops: camisoles

A trench coat

George Simonton:

A little black dress

A magnificent white shirt

A great-fitting pair of pants (straight-leg)

A fabulous black pantsuit

A slim pencil skirt, grazing the knee

A six-gore boot-length knit or gabardine skirt, fitted around the stomach

Great-fitting jeans

A classic black turtleneck, preferably cashmere

Tops: camisoles, tank tops, and T-shirts

A cashmere twin set

A classic blazer

A jacket, quilted barn jacket, or anorak

A trench coat

A good winter coat

The Well-Edited Wardrobe for Men

Once upon a time, businessmen wore suits to work. And that was that. But in the wake of "casual Fridays," and less stringent dress regulations in general, men's wardrobe essentials are not so simple anymore. As a result, men have more fashion options today. Although the suit is still a staple (the necktie is now a fashion statement for young men), there are other essential items that a modern man needs in his wardrobe. Below is a list of the classics that go with everything, that look and feel good no matter how often they are worn. According to leading men's fashion experts, the essentials for a man's wardrobe are:

A good-quality wool suit

A single-breasted navy blazer

An assortment of cotton shirts

A good-quality knit tie

A pair of well-cut straight-leg dark denim jeans

A pair of well-cut cotton chinos

A good-quality sweater

A sport coat

A trench coat

A jacket (depending on climate)

Men's Essentials: What the Experts Say

With dress codes relaxing over the last decade, the wardrobe rules have changed for men. Here, fashion pros offer their opinions on the must-haves:

*A **good-quality wool suit**.* Though the suit may be less of a requirement in the workplace, it is still an essential in a man's wardrobe. The majority of the experts say the best all-around colors are gray, navy, and black.

A solid-gray flannel single-breasted suit is a classic, says Michael Bastian, a menswear designer, creative director for menswear at Bill Blass, and former fashion director of Bergdorf Goodman Men. "Get it in an appropriate weight for where you live and you can wear it as a suit or break it up and wear the pants alone or the jacket alone with jeans."

"A gray suit is a Cary Grant classic that has returned to

prominence," says Dirk Standen, the editor in chief of Style. com and Men.Style.com. "It may even be more essential than a navy suit at this point." He recommends a two-button wool suit. "Freemans Sporting Club does a great classic cut, using deadstock wools, and their suits are handmade in Brooklyn, which you can't say about the average Savile Row suit."

Michael Macko, men's fashion director at Saks Fifth Avenue, says a medium-gray suit in worsted wool is a good choice. He also thinks men need a black suit. "A good black suit will carry you through 99 percent of dressy occasions. Most events now are black-tie optional or fancy dress, so a black suit can double as a tuxedo. Just make sure your shirt is white and crisp."

Navy blue is the preferred all-around suit color for Simon Doonan, creative director of Barneys New York and the author of *Eccentric Glamour: Creating an Insanely More Fabulous You* and *Confessions of a Window Dresser.* "A navy lightweight wool suit is the most useful garment in the universe," he says. "You can wear the pants with everything, even a denim jacket. And the jacket makes a great classic sport coat."

If you have to dress for work: The experts say you need at least three to five suits. "A business dude needs five sharp suits in his closet," says Doonan. "Most guys are very messy eaters. They are rough on their clothes. It's all about rotation, ditto shirts, shoes, and ties." He recommends two navy suits: one solid, one striped; two dark gray suits: one solid, one striped; and one black suit—all in lightweight fabrics. Michael Bastian thinks a man needs "at least three or four good suits, five maximum. You need a solid gray, a solid navy, a pinstripe in gray or navy, and a good tan cotton summer suit."

*A **single-breasted navy blazer.*** This basic is on almost every expert's list. "It is still one of the most essential things in a man's wardrobe," says Michael Macko. "It's so old school and classic, but it really can take you anywhere. You can wear it over jeans, white pants, chinos, or gray pants from your suit." But stay away from metal buttons. "Unless you're in the habit of being addressed as commodore, stick with regular buttons rather than brass," says Dirk Standen. His recommendation: "Ralph Lauren Black Label has a nice slim fit."

*An **assortment of cotton shirts.*** The white dress shirt is a classic on everyone's list. "Some days a white shirt is the only thing that makes me look half alive," says Standen. "I like Prada because the fabrics and cuts have a modern feel that's not too stuffy. After white I'd go pink and then blue." Bastian agrees. "You need a perfect white shirt, a perfect blue shirt, and a perfect pink shirt."

Those classics are also on Macko's list, but he says shirts are a category where men can really show off their style sense. "Guys can have a lot of fun with dress shirts," he says. "Most guys love uniforms. They tend to think shirts only come in blue and white. Of course, you can be perfectly well dressed in a navy blazer, blue shirt, and a pair of gray pants. But you can go from well dressed to fashionable by substituting a burgundy-and-white Bengal stripe, a gingham, a plaid, a microcheck, or something with contrasting collar and cuff."

Macko says, if given the choice between a dress or a sport shirt, go for the dress shirt. "Dress shirts are much more versatile and you'll get more mileage out of them. Most sport shirts are sized small, medium, large, and extra large. Dress shirts are available in your appropriate sleeve length and neck size so you're going to get a much better fit. You can wear a dress shirt with a tie or as a sport shirt, whereas a sport shirt is not designed to be worn with a tie and it's not going to look right if you do because the neck is going to be either too tight or too large."

If you have to dress for work: The experts say have at least fifteen dress shirts in your wardrobe. Why so many? Rotation, rotation, rotation. "I don't know how often you do laundry, but figure that you're always going to have at least five shirts out of commission," says Bastian. Doonan also recommends fifteen shirts: five simple stripes, five blue solids, and five whites.

A good-quality knit tie. "Buy a good navy blue cashmere tie and it will get you through 90 percent of situations you will need a tie for," says Bastian. Macko prefers the Charvet black knit tie. "Ties tend to accumulate in guys' wardrobes—they're the hardest things to edit down. I still have ties from high school," he says.

If you have to dress for work: "You need at least five good ties at minimum," says Macko. "They should be in a palette that works within your wardrobe. So if you have a navy blazer and gray suit, get ties in burgundy, navy, rep stripes, maybe even a little gold. They should all work withinthe same colors. Don't get too elaborate with patterns and colors—pattern-mixing is not for the faint of heart."

A pair of well-cut dark-denim straight-leg jeans. This is a must-have on almost every expert's list. "Look for a narrow fit but one that's not too skinny, a waist that's not too low," says Standen. "Rag & Bone usually deliver, though the Levi's 501 is still hard to beat. I don't worry too much about selvedge and all that. Life's too short." Macko is also a fan of the Levi's 501 classic. "It's a straight leg but not a super-skinny jean. Guys don't want a skinny jean because they don't want to look like they're wearing girls' jeans." He says avoid the boot cut. "There's a lot of excess fabric—there's no reason to walk on the back of your jeans or to have them ripped at the bottom. There should be a little break above the shoe."

Because jeans are so comfortable, some guys may tend to wear them a little too often. Avoid that if you can, Standen says. "You shouldn't over-rely on jeans, which is why at least twice a year I try to wear a pair of cords."

A pair of well-cut chinos. Another essential in the modern man's wardrobe. "Khakis are a great denim alternative," says Macko. "They should be clean, fit well, and be pressed, especially for working. They look great with a navy blazer or gray suit jacket." He recommends having two pair—one for work and a more casual pair for the weekend.

A good-quality sweater. "A gray V-neck always looks smart but understated," says Standen. "I have one in cotton from Martin Margiela that's the perfect weight and cut, with suede elbow patches in camel. I keep hoping it'll last another winter." Bastian also likes the V-neck and the crew neck in navy cashmere. And Doonan and Macko are fans of zip-front cardigans.

A sport coat. A sport coat is another versatile item in your wardrobe because it can be dressed up or down. "In a weird way it has become the new coat," says Bastian. "These days the weather is so unpredictable. If you live in New York, for instance, you don't really need a heavy coat until the snow starts. A good tweed jacket—along with scarf, gloves, and hat—can get you through to the first snowstorm. It's all about the accessories." Doonan thinks a man needs two sport coats: one in tweed, the other in cotton.

A trench coat. This is another tried and true basic on most experts' lists. Bastian says you can't go wrong with a Burberry. Macko agrees. "It's probably one of the most versatile outerwear pieces you can have. It's classic, timeless," he says. "Buy one with a removable lining and you can wear it all year round, without the lining in the spring, and with the lining in fall and winter."

A jacket. Whether you need outerwear depends on the climate you live in. "Leather or suede to me are too fussy, but a cotton bomber jacket is a modern classic that always makes me feel like Steve McQueen—even if I don't know one end of a motorcycle from the other," says Standen. Macko likes the bomber jacket and is also a fan of the classic navy peacoat.

Rules to Dress By, According to the Experts

Michael Bastian:

1. Buy less but buy better. Americans have this concept of cutting corners on basic stuff. But I think you should spend the most you can afford on the stuff you wear every day. A good piece of clothing may hurt upfront, but in the end you'll spend less than on all that cheap stuff you never wear and throw out. When you buy good clothing, it gives you a little bit of pleasure when you put it on because it makes you look and feel great.

2. Get your suit tailored to fit your body. The biggest mistake that American men make is that as a rule they buy their suits one size too big. The suit jacket should have some relation to your body. Also, try on a few different sizes—don't just stick to the size you think you are. Not all manufacturers' sizes fit the same.

3. Don't wear cheap shoes. Some guys will spend the money on a good suit and shirt, and they'll have a great haircut. But then you look down and they're wearing a cheap pair of square-toed loafers. And it just ruins the whole look.

4. Think about proportion. The width of your tie should reflect the width of your lapel. If you have a narrow-lapel jacket, you need a narrow tie. If your jacket has a wide lapel, you need a wider tie. It's the same with collar length. A small collar doesn't look good with a double-breasted peak-lapel suit. It also applies to shoes. A big baggy pleated pant needs a heavier shoe to anchor it.

5. Don't wear a tie with a short-sleeved shirt. I can see the nerdy appeal of it, but in general, in the wrong hands it's an easy no.

6. Don't wear a denim jacket with denim jeans. I have yet to figure out a cool way to wear a denim jacket with jeans.

The problem is it always has that denim leisure suit look. It just never looks good.

7. Don't wear ankle-length short socks. Wear over-the-calf socks or don't wear socks at all.

Simon Doonan:

1. Dress appropriately for the kind of work you do. I work in fashion so I can do whatever the hell I want. However, most guys need to dress in a way which exudes competence and stability, especially if they are handling large sums of money or medical instruments. Nobody wants a colonoscopy performed by some guy wearing the latest trendy Dolce & Gabbana outfit.

2. Keep it simple. The key for most men is to get organized. Don't feel guilty about having a uniform way of dressing.

Michael Macko:

1. Find a good tailor, whether it's someone at the store where you purchase your clothes or an independent tailor. Tailoring is essential—your clothes should fit you perfectly.

2. Break up your suit. Look at the pants and jacket as two separate pieces. If you have a gray suit, for instance, you can wear the jacket with a pair of khakis or wear the pants with a navy blazer.

3. Think of your wardrobe as a whole unit. Before adding a piece, think about how it will work with your other clothes. Also, avoid the impulsive sale item purchase. Before you buy that rust-color sport coat, you have to think, "How will this fit in with my mostly navy and gray wardrobe?"

4. If you need help with your wardrobe, establish a relationship with a sales associate at a store you shop in regularly. That person can help you find the right fit and help fill in the gaps.

5. Match socks to your suit. A common mistake is that men buy just black socks and wear them with everything. If you're wearing a gray suit, wear gray socks. Also, match your belt to your shoes.

6. Find the best dry cleaner you can. Limit cleaning to no more than twice a season. Dry-cleaning chemicals can be harsh on some fabrics, and too much pressing can make a suit look shiny. Always dry clean before you put a seasonal wardrobe away because food, oil, or perspiration stains will attract moths.

7. Invest in shoe trees. They will significantly extend the life of your shoes. Buy unvarnished cedar—it absorbs moisture and odors.

Dirk Standen:

1. Buy clothes that fit (not two sizes too large or one size too small).

2. Stick to navy, gray, white, shades of blue, a bit of camel, and a shot of pink.

3. Buy one expensive thing and wear it again and again rather than five cheaper things. (You can tell people it's your uniform.)

4. Have the illusion of health. JFK knew that. The guy had an almost crippling back condition, but with that tan and that great hair he always managed to convey the impression of vitality.

The Insiders: Their Top Choices

Men's fashion experts, like women's, don't agree on every clothing essential. The master list (mentioned previously) was compiled from their personal choices. Here are their lists:

Michael Bastian:

A gray flannel suit (at least three to five suits if you have to dress for work)

A good pair of cotton chinos

A single-breasted navy blazer

A navy cashmere sweater, either V-neck or crew

Good cotton oxford cloth shirts, white, blue, or pink

A good navy cashmere tie

A perfect-fitting pair of jeans

A trench coat

A herringbone-tweed Shetland-wool jacket

Simon Doonan:

A navy lightweight wool suit (if you have to dress for work, at least five suits—two navy, striped and solid; two dark gray, striped and solid; one black)

At least fifteen dress shirts (if you have to dress for work—five simple stripes, five blue solids, and five white)

Five sport shirts: two check and three solid, in different weights

Three pairs of chinos or jeans

A zip-front sweater

Two sport coats: one cotton and one tweed

Michael Macko:

Two suits, medium-gray and black, worsted wool (weight depends on climate)

A single-breasted navy blazer

About eight to ten cotton shirts (dress and sport)

A good black knit tie (at least five ties if you have to dress for work)

A pair of well-cut chinos

A pair of straight-leg dark denim jeans

A zip-front or button-front sweater, in cashmere or merino wool

A trench coat

A tweed sport coat

A peacoat or bomber-style jacket (if you live in a cooler climate)

Dirk Standen:

A single-breasted navy blazer

A gray single-breasted, two-button wool suit

A light gray V-neck sweater, in cotton or fine-gauge cashmere

A pair of straight-leg dark denim jeans

A white cotton shirt

A black cotton zip-front bomber jacket

{necessary luxuries for women}

Items to Splurge On. Not everything in your wardrobe has to be top-of-the-line. You can cut corners on things like pants, skirts, and underpinnings. "To me, those are backdrop clothes. You can get reasonably well-fitting pants and skirts in many designers' secondary lines," says George Simonton, professor of fashion design at the Fashion Institute of Technology, in New York. But you should go for top quality on these items:

Shoes. "There's nothing worse than a cheap pair of shoes," said Jasmine H. Chang, executive fashion editor of *O: The Oprah Magazine.* "I'm not saying you have to spend $600 on a pair of shoes. I don't. I'm talking about those cheesy knockoffs. They look bad and hurt, to boot." Simonton agrees: "Your shoes should be good quality. A friend of mine years ago would spend a fortune on her clothing but would buy cheap shoes—it really could spoil the entire look."

Handbag. "Every woman needs at least one real status bag, if nothing for self-esteem," says Chang. "A great designer handbag holds that power."

"It doesn't have to be the bag of the season," says the fashion designer Dana Buchman, "but you should have one good bag."

A jacket and a winter coat (depending on climate). Tailoring and fit really count here, says Buchman. "Spend the most on a jacket. Fine tailoring shows up in the shoulders, in the folds of the lapel, and in the hang of the garment. A great jacket hangs beautifully from the shoulder—it has to fit you from the shoulder."

A great white shirt. "The great white shirt should not be compromised," says Chang. "Spend the most you can afford."

Going for the Gold. Buying high-end designer clothing or accessories is certainly not essential. On the other hand, your money will not be wasted if you know what to look for. A good-quality classic will give you years of wearing pleasure and can also be a smart investment that will increase in value. "A few necessary luxuries go a long way," says Glenda Bailey, editor in chief of *Harper's Bazaar.* "Your accountant may never understand why it's an essential investment, but that's why she's in finance. The price of fashion goes up every year, so buying now can save you money."

If you decide to go haute couture, Bailey says, "buy labels that will increase in value, like Hermès, Lanvin, Louis Vuitton, YSL, and Chanel. Don't cut the labels out, and be sure to keep magazine coverage referring to your pieces: they are your insurance policy for resale."

Also, she says, "calculate cost per wear. That $1,000 bag that you will use twice a week for the next ten years—costing you less than a dollar per wear—is better than a one-season wonder."

Dana Buchman says evening bags are another great fashion investment. "They are timeless. You can pass them down to your daughters. They never go out of style." 🡕

{on bras and bathing suits}

The Perfect Bra. The right foundation garments can make all the difference, says Glenda Bailey. "Seven out of ten women are wearing the wrong size bra." You can find the right fit in two easy steps: "Measure under your bust at your rib cage, around your back and under your arms, and add 5 (round out if necessary) to get your band size. Then measure across the fullest part of your bust and subtract the number from step one for your cup size: 0 = AA; 1 = A; 2 = B; 3 = C; 4 = D; 5 = DD."

The Perfect Bathing Suit. For many women, buying a bathing suit can be an annual trauma. What's the best color to minimize a less-than-perfect figure? It's solid black, right? Wrong, says the fashion designer Nicole Miller. If you want to hide any flaws, don't wear solid black or pastel bathing suits, she advises. "Print bathing suits are much more camouflaging and make you look thinner than black suits. Pastel suits are even worse than black.

Prints are much more forgiving—they take the focus away. When you wear a black or pastel suit, you can't hide anything." ⬀

{accessories: women's must-haves}

Accessories, says George Simonton, "can make or break an outfit. Good pieces of jewelry, a great watch, shoes, and handbag can make all the difference." Here are some insider recommendations:

Shoes. "A high-heel pump, perfect flats, and evening sandals," says Glenda Bailey.

"A fabulous pair of black pumps," says Simonton.

"A pair of flat boots, a pair of great shoes that give you some height—it could be killer pumps, wedge, or platform," says Jasmine H. Chang. "I also love men's-style oxford flats and ballet shoes by Repetto."

"A pair of the highest heels you can possibly walk

in," says Dana Buchman. "They look phenomenal. They're bad for your feet and they hurt, but they're worth it."

"Open-toe shoes in the summer," says Nicole Miller. "Early in the season, when your legs aren't tanned yet, buy a pair of neutral-color shoes—like tan suede or antique gold. Those colors are much more forgiving than black."

Handbag. Across the board, all the experts say every woman needs at least one great handbag.

Jewelry. "A great watch speaks a thousand words," says Chang.

"You need a good basic necklace that goes with everything," says Miller. "You also need some pieces with antique finishes on gold or silver."

"Diamond stud earrings—they look chic with everything," says Buchman. "And it doesn't matter if they're real or fake."

"A great watch," says Simonton.

Belts. "A fabulous leather or suede belt," says Simonton. "A belt can really change the entire look of an outfit." ✒

{accessories: men's must-haves}

All the experts agree that men should limit accessories. "Keep it to a minimum," says Simon Doonan, creative director of Barneys New York. "Don't fool around with pocket squares and cuff links unless you are a dandy and you really know what you are doing." The accessories that count are:

Shoes. "A good pair of cordovan laceups or slip-ons," says the designer Michael Bastian, creative director of menswear at Bill Blass. "Guys have to think about shoes the way they think about a car—it's an investment. Cordovans are almost impossible to destroy. You can resole them twenty times and have them your whole life."

"For work you need black wingtips and some simple black slip-ons, which are styled-down versions of Prada shoes from ten seasons ago," says Doonan.

"Black or brown Chelsea boots," says Dirk Standen, editor in chief of Style.com and Men.Style.com. "I hate laces and I'm not a big fan of socks. In summer I wear loafers or Vans. In winter it's Chelsea boots—at least you don't see the socks."

"A pair of dressy black laceups, chocolate brown suede laceups or slip-ons, a great pair of sneakers, and black or chocolate brown Chelsea boots," says Michael Macko, men's fashion diector at Saks Fifth Avenue.

Watch. "Get the best one you can afford," Bastian says. Standen agrees. "Accessories are one of the first things people notice. You can wear fairly basic clothes but spend the money on a decent watch. An architect friend of mine has this expression—'the richer the client, the cheaper the watch'—and most of us aren't rich enough to wear a cheap watch." He recommends a "stainless-steel Rolex GMT Master, with black bezel and black dial. You're either a Rolex guy or you're not. These days I wear a gold Daytona, which I'm not sure you can call strictly essential, but every day for twenty years, I wore a steel GMT Master. I think it's a marginally subtler watch than the Submariner."

Belt. "You need a black and a brown belt," says Macko. "I'm a follower of the belt-should-match-your-shoes school. Hermès has a reversible belt and a lot of designers like Ferragamo and Gucci offer belts in the same material as their shoes."

Hat. This depends on your climate, of course. "A tweed flat cap," says Standen. "There's not much point to losing your hair if you can't wear the occasional bit of jaunty headgear. I like to think a tweed cap gives me that devil-may-care, John Huston-in-Ireland flair, and it keeps my head warm." Macko thinks you can't go wrong with a navy or black cashmere knit cap. ⚑

{out with the old: taming your closet}

Have you lost control of your clothes closet? You're not alone, says Peter Walsh, of TLC's *Clean Sweep* and author of *It's All Too Much: An Easy Plan for Living a Richer Life with Less Stuff*. The trouble: We buy too much.

"I honestly believe, and I use this term deliberately, that we are in an orgy of consumption," he says. "The reasons? Largely, stuff is cheap, credit is easy. We live in a culture that says more is better—if one is good, then two must be better. It's the supersize mentality. We live in a culture that also says success is measured by the acquisition of goods. Finally, and I think this is the worst reason of all, we are caught up in buying not the product but the promise. When we buy a pair of jeans, we buy the promise that if we put them on, our butts will look smaller."

How do you feel when you look in your closet—confused, depressed, guilty? When you're facing racks of clothing you no longer wear or like, it's hard to find what you're looking for. It can also be an emotional minefield loaded with reminders of the past—of weight gained or not lost; money spent unwisely; or even relationships gone awry. Letting go of excess stuff can be cathartic, clearing the mind and revitalizing the spirit by making way for new things.

To help you eliminate distracting clothes, Walsh offers a basic rule: "If you haven't worn an item in twelve months, ask yourself, 'Do I really need it?' " Of course, use common sense here; the rule may not apply to special items—if you own a beautiful one-of-a-kind Balenciaga gown, for instance—or seasonal wear—ski clothing or a winter coat.

Also, Walsh advises, toss out any clothes that cause emotional turmoil. "Women's closets are full of 'wish' clothes, which exist for only one reason: to mock you," he says. "Get rid of them. If you're on a sensible diet-and-exercise program, when you get down to your ideal weight, then go buy a couple of outfits that look good and fit you."

In addition, clear out the pricey "fashion mistake" clothes, the ones that never looked good on you even though you paid a king's ransom for them. "Do you want a closet full of clothes that make you feel guilty every time you look at them?" says Walsh.

Discard the clothes with negative associations—if a certain green dress always reminds you of your first date with your cheating ex-boyfriend, then toss it.

If you're not sure about how often you wear certain items, Walsh offers a simple strategy to keep track. "Turn all your hangers in your closet back to front," he says. "For the next few months, when you wear an item and hang it up, put the hanger back in the correct way. At the end of six to nine months, if you find hangers that are still back to front, what are they doing in your closet?"

In the end, Walsh says, you should think of your closet in terms of a relationship. "The overriding thing is that you first have to honor and respect the space limitations your closet places on you—in the same way you have to honor and respect a person in a relationship. If you don't honor and respect the space limitations of your closet, it will turn on you like a bad lover. It's true. People will say, 'My closet drives me crazy. I feel suffocated when I go in there.' Are we talking about your closet or a bad relationship? It's the same thing." ⌞

{greening your closet}

We all remember that iconic scene in the 1981 movie *Mommie Dearest* when Joan Crawford (played by the actress Faye Dunaway) has a meltdown over wire hangers in her daughter's closet. If you share Crawford's particular aversion, think before you toss your hangers in the trash. Though wire hangers are recyclable, the majority of them (in the billions) wind up in landfills every year. The problem: Not all communities recycle hangers.

Before you discard your hangers, ask your dry cleaner if he or she will accept returns. If they don't, check with local churches, homeless shelters, or charitable groups that run thrift stores (like the Salvation Army) to see if they need hangers.

Another alternative is to ask your dry cleaner about using paper hangers. A company called Hanger Network has created EcoHangers, which are made from 100 percent recycled paper and are biodegradable. The company is trying to get more dry cleaners to use EcoHangers, which are distributed free to businesses in a variety of cities around the country.

One more eco-closet tip: When storing your winter clothing, don't use mothballs. They are made of paradichlorobenzene or naphthalene, toxic chemicals associated with a host of physical ailments, including irritation of the skin, throat, and eyes. For an eco-friendly alternative, use cedar products, eucalyptus, or lavender. ⬀

{are you an ecofashionista?}

If you are, then you know that green is the new black. More designers and companies are offering earth-friendly clothing made with organic fabrics (containing no harmful chemicals, made from materials grown without pesticides) and manufactured in factories with worker-friendly conditions. Here are some eco-hip sites:

Americanapparel.com

Beklina.com

Bluecanoe.com

Coolnotcruel.com

Earthspeaks.com

Gaiam.com

Genopalette.com

Indigenousdesigns.com

Loomstate.org

Maggiesorganics.com

Oftheearth.com

Patagonia.com

Rawganique.com

Thegreenloop.com

Underthecanopy.com

Utopianliving.com

Vegetarian-shoes.co.uk

Wildlifeworks.com

If you want to be an environmentally friendly shopper, invest in reusable tote bags to carry home your treasures. Check out Doy bags (doybags.com), made from recycled juice packs, nonbiodegradable foil, and plastic packaging; Minus bags (minusbags.com), made from 100 percent cotton; and Reusablebags.com, which offer a full range of fabric and string bags.

{when too much is not enough}

It's no secret: Shopping is an American pastime. And that's okay—if you can afford it. But too much retail therapy can wreak havoc on your finances—and your personal life. A closet overflowing with the latest Jimmy Choos and Chloé dresses will be little comfort if your electricity is being turned off for lack of payment or your wages are being garnished by your creditors.

According to some estimates, more than 10 million (some say as high as 60 million) Americans are compulsive buyers and spenders. Experts say one of the reasons we buy too much stuff we don't need is the availability of easy credit. Credit card debt has soared from $238 billion in 1989 to $800 billion in 2005, according to Demos, a research and consumer advocacy organization. It is estimated that the average American family now owes about $9,000 in credit card debt.

If you are drowning in debt and/or spending beyond your means, you can get help from Debtors Anonymous (debtorsanonymous.org). Based on the model for Alcoholics Anonymous, this is a twelve-step program for people who have any kind of money issues—whether it's credit card debt, overspending, shopping, or underearning. DA offers meetings across the country and around the world. Through support from others in the program, you will learn how to manage your money and become solvent.

If you are considering going to a credit counselor, do your homework first (some services may be less than honorable). These government agencies offer solid information:

The Federal Trade Commission (ftc.gov/bcp/conline/pubs/credit/fiscal.shtm) offers good advice about finding the right credit counseling organization, questions to ask, and so on.

The Department of Justice (usdoj.gov/ust/eo/bapcpa/ccde/index.htm) offers a list of approved counseling services around the country. ⧉

{clothes consciousness}

Want to pare down your closet, do a good deed, and help the earth by not filling up the landfills (where, by the way, most of our used clothing winds up)? Many charitable organizations around the country will gladly accept donations of used clothing, and you also get a tax deduction for your generosity. Here are some worthy groups:

Dress for Success (dressforsuccess.org) and The Women's Alliance (thewomensalliance.org) are nonprofit groups that accept donations of gently used business clothing, which is given to women in financial need who are trying to get jobs in the corporate world.

The Princess Project (princessproject.org) and the Glass Slipper Project (glassslipperproject.org) are nonprofit groups, located in San Francisco and Chicago, respectively. They are two of several organizations around the country that accept donations of prom dresses, formal gowns, or party dresses, which are given free to high school girls in need. Their websites provide links for other groups around the country.

The Salvation Army (salvationarmyusa.org) accepts used clothing as well as many other household items. You can drop off donations at designated centers near you; you can also arrange for pickups from your home. Check the website for a branch near you.

Goodwill Industries International (goodwill.org) accepts clothing, furniture, and appliances at thousands of drop-off locations around the country. Check the website for a branch near you.

The Society of St. Vincent de Paul (svdpusa.org)

accepts donations of clothing and other household items at thrift stores located all over the United States. Check the website for a branch near you.

Clothes Off Our Back (clothesoffourback.org). If you want to buy high-end clothes and contribute to a worthy cause at the same time, this nonprofit organization (founded by the actors Jane Kaczmarek and Bradley Whitford) sponsors auctions of clothing and accessories donated by big-name celebrities and designers, with proceeds going to various children's charities. You can bid on A-lister apparel or donate money. 🖱

A Roof over Your Head: Shelter and Safety

Simplicity is the ultimate sophistication.

—LEONARDO DA VINCI

A friend who writes about design recently described to me a new home he had visited. The house, built for a couple with two children, was 27,000 square feet and had a $40 million price tag. Among its thirty-five-plus rooms were his and hers libraries, a gift-wrapping room, a flower-arranging room, a potting room, a wine-tasting room (next to the wine cellar, of course), a movie theater with a candy store, a massage room (next to the sauna and gym), and countless cavernous closets (one just for belts).

In recent years much has been written about living simply. Yet our houses seem to be getting bigger and bigger. According to the National Association of Homebuilders, the average single-family home in the United States in 2004 was 2,349 square feet—quite a jump when you consider that in 1950 it was 983 square feet.

What do we really need in a living space? When you pare it down, the essential rooms in a home are the ones that revolve around our basic needs—eating, bathing/grooming, and sleeping. The essential rooms are:

The kitchen
The bathroom
The bedroom

Our Other Basic Need: Safety

The essential rooms—especially the kitchen and the bathroom—are among the most trafficked in the home. The bedroom may not get as much daytime traffic, but according to some sleep experts, the bed is the most utilized piece of furniture in the house (don't forget that you spend a third of your life sleeping).

Because we use the essential rooms frequently, they should be not only aesthetically pleasing and functional but also safe. After the automobile, the home is the most common location for unintentional injury–related deaths; the kitchen and the bathroom are among the most dangerous rooms in the home. About 20,000 deaths and 21 million medical visits a year can be attributed to home-based accidents in this country, according to the Home Safety Council, a nonprofit organization dedicated to preventing home injuries.

For this reason, the must-haves for kitchen, bathroom, and bedroom are a mix of functional and safety items.

Kitchen Essentials: What the Experts Say

No room evokes sentiments of home like the kitchen. The aromas of cooking or baking can jog our deepest memories associated with comfort and warmth. Food—the sustenance of life—is synonymous with love.

For these reasons and more the kitchen—the place where we prepare and cook food—is the most dominant room in the home. And it has become even more so over the last fifteen to twenty years, with the explosion of interest in all things culinary related.

"I think what has happened is that the kitchen has become the new living room," says celebrity chef Marcus Samuelsson, author of *The Soul of a New Cuisine*, host of *Inner Chef* on the Discovery Home Channel, and chef and coowner of Aquavit restaurant in New York City.

It's true. Our kitchens have become showplaces—not only

are they functional rooms for cooking, they also are social settings for dining and entertaining. As a result, we spend a lot of money remodeling them—$127.1 billion in 2006, according to the National Kitchen and Bath Association.

The kitchen has become so popular that many people no longer use their dining rooms, says lifestyle expert Susie Coelho, host of *Outer Spaces* on HGTV, product designer, and author of *Secrets of a Style Diva: A Get Inspired Guide to Your Creative Side* and *Style Your Dream Wedding*. "Kitchens are no longer kitchens—they've become a meeting place for family and friends," says Coelho. "Most people I know don't eat in their formal dining rooms anymore. In fact, they've converted their dining rooms into more practical spaces—offices, playrooms, studios, or workout rooms. I converted mine into a family room."

Our styles of entertaining have become more casual, Coelho observes. "The kitchen is definitely the fun place to hang out while the host or hostess is cooking. To me that's the best kind of dinner party. It's so much more social to have everyone in the kitchen talking and contributing—one person makes the salad dressing, while another person pours the wine. That's much more fun than hanging out in a stuffy living room drinking cocktails while the host or hostess is cooking in the kitchen. That's how people live now."

To outfit our showplace kitchens, we spend a lot of money buying cookware—$2.2 billion in 2006, reports the Cookware Manufacturers Association. But do we need to fill our kitchens with a lot of high-end equipment? And if not, what are the essentials we really need to cook well?

To find out, I interviewed five top chefs: Marcus Samuelsson; Ina Garten, host of *Barefoot Contessa* on the Food Network and author of *The Barefoot Contessa Cookbook* and *Barefoot Contessa at Home*; Sara Moulton, host of *Sara's Secrets* on the Food Network, executive chef of *Gourmet* magazine, food editor of *Good Morning America,* and author of *Sara's Secrets for Weeknight Meals* and *Sara Moulton Cooks at Home*; Ming Tsai, host of *Simply Ming* on PBS, author of *Simply Ming, Blue Ginger,* and *Ming's Master Recipes*, and owner of Blue Ginger, and East/West Bistro in Wellesley, Massachusetts; Rick Bayless, host of *Mexico: One Plate at a Time* on PBS, author of *Mexican Everyday* and *Rick and Lanie's Excellent Kitchen Adventures*, and owner of Frontera Grill in Chicago.

According to America's top chefs, the essentials for cooking well are:

3 knives: a 10- or 12-inch chef's knife, a paring knife, and a serrated knife (all made of good-quality material)

Assortment of wooden spoons, a ladle, and a slotted spoon

Heatproof rubber spatula

Whisk (medium to large)

Tongs (long and short)

Skillet or sauté pan: 10- or 12-inch (good-quality heavy metal)

Saucepans with lids, all good-quality heavy metal: small (about 2 quart), medium (about 4 quart), and large (about 6 to 8 quarts—can be used for making stock or pasta)

Rimmed baking sheets (12 by 18 inches)

Set of stainless-steel nesting bowls

Cutting board: wooden or bamboo

Set of measuring spoons

2 glass measuring cups: 2 cup and 4 cup

Colander and medium-size mesh strainer

Peeler with a good grip

Cheese grater or Microplane (mandolin optional)

Thermometer (instant-read)

Can opener

Knife sharpener

For baking: two pie/cake pans, a muffin tin, a loaf pan for quick breads, and a rolling pin

Food processor (good-quality)

Hand mixer (a standing mixer is great if you can afford it, but not necessary)

Blender (optional)

Overall Tips from Top Chefs

Before buying anything, chefs say you first must evaluate how often you cook, how many people you cook for, and what sort of cooking you do. For instance, if you never bake, don't waste your money on baking supplies. Here are some tips from the pros:

Knives, saucepans, and skillets. You do not have to spend a lot of money on kitchen equipment, professional chefs say. But there are two categories where quality counts most, and then there is everything else. "You need two or three really good knives and two or three really good pots and pans," says Marcus Samuelsson.

After that, chefs say that the rest of your equipment doesn't have to be top-of-the-line stuff (hint: for good deals and a variety of choices, go to a restaurant supply store— that's where the pros shop).

"Spend the most money on your knives and pots and pans," says Sara Moulton. "Why? Because you'll have them for the rest of your life. You don't have to spend a lot of money on the rest. The difference between a heavy-gauge good pot and a thin cheap pot is huge in terms of the end result. The difference between expensive or cheap spoons and bowls is minuscule."

"I've had some of my knives for the entire time I've been cooking and that's 30 years," says Ina Garten.

Knives should be made of a good-quality, very hard material that will maintain a sharp edge. Ming Tsai uses ceramic knives made by Kyocera. "I love them because they keep their edge for the longest time and they are also very light, which I like because it tends to get less tiring."

A sharp knife is critical. "The most dangerous thing in your home kitchen is a dull knife, not a sharp knife," says Tsai. "If you're cutting a tomato or an orange, for instance, a dull knife will slip and that's when you cut yourself."

He also uses a Chinese cleaver as a multipurpose chef's knife. "I love a good old-fashioned Chinese cleaver," he says. "It's the best not only for chopping things up but it's fantastic for picking things off the board and putting them into your pot or pan because it's got a good surface area. And it's also great for hacking up bones. It's the most durable knife out there."

Pots and pans should have heft (weightiness), be easy to handle and sturdy, and be made of good-quality metals that distribute heat evenly. "Pots and pans need to be a minimum of three ply and preferably five ply," says Tsai. (Ply refers to layers of metal.)

"I'm all for cast-iron, especially a skillet," says Moulton. "The more you use it, as long as you treat it well, the more nonstick it becomes. The interesting thing about cast iron is that it takes longer to heat up, but once you heat it up, it maintains its heat evenly and beautifully."

When buying knives or cookware, professional chefs say avoid packaged sets. "I never buy sets of pots and pans because they always include things that you never use," says Garten. "My advice is to buy one really good-quality pot instead of buying a whole set of medium-quality things. And then every year, for Christmas or your birthday, just add one more thing."

"I don't buy complete sets of pots or skillets," says Samuelsson. "I buy pieces that work for how I cook."

When buying skillets, consider a larger size over a smaller one. "I use a 12-inch skillet the most," says Rick Bayless. "Most people use the 10-inch, but I think it crowds food and I can't get the kind of sear on food that I like."

Cooks often make the mistake of overfilling the pan. "When people cook, the most common error they make is when they overstuff a sauté pan or a wok," says Tsai. "If you put too much into a pan, you cannot maintain the heat and you won't get the sear or caramelization or quick stir-fry effect you want. So I always recommend, even in my recipes, to put half the amount in." (Note: A wok is essential if you do Asian-style cooking, Tsai says.)

Baking sheets and roasting pans. Baking (cookie) sheets are extremely versatile. "I have about six half-sheet pans, and they're probably the best investment in equipment I've ever made," says Garten. "I don't think I paid more than $10 or $15 for them. I use them for everything—roasting, baking, and baking cookies."

If you do a lot of roasting, Moulton and Tsai both recommend investing in a good roasting pan. "A heavy-duty roasting pan with a V-rack is great," says Moulton.

"My favorite thing is a roasting pan—you can just throw your vegetables and chicken in it and in an hour or so your dinner is ready," says Tsai.

Stainless-steel bowls. Chefs say that inexpensive stainless-steel bowls are another must-have because they can do double duty for many cooking chores. "I love stainless-steel nesting bowls because they're extremely durable," says Bayless. "You don't need to worry about breaking them. You can put them over a pot of boiling water if you want to heat something up."

Thermometers and ovens. One common cooking problem is how to gauge heat in the oven.

"One thing I think is essential is an oven thermometer because what your dial says usually bears no relationship to the temperature of the oven," says Garten.

Of course, a good-quality stove can make a big difference. "The heart and soul of every kitchen, I think, is a great stove," says Samuelsson, who uses a BlueStar stove in his kitchen. "Regardless of the brand, the things you want to know are how does it transfer heat? Does it give you the highest BTUs [British thermal units]? How does the oven draw heat? How quickly does it go to 400 degrees? Do you have to go to 450 degrees to get to 400? When it is at 400, does it go down to 325 when you open it, or do you lose only 5 degrees?"

Appliances. Most chefs agree that a good-quality food processor is an essential in the kitchen these days, but a blender is in the optional category, depending on what you cook. "There are certainly things that they both do about the same, but when it comes to getting a really creamy puree or a really creamy soup, you're not going to get that in a food processor," says Moulton. "You have to use a blender."

Garten says that when she makes soups and sauces, she prefers using an old-fashioned food mill. "Food processors end up too smooth for me. I like soups with a lot of texture, so if I'm making a butternut squash and apple soup, for instance, I put it through the food mill. It gives the soup more body."

Kitchen Safety Essentials: What the Experts Say

Kitchens evoke warm and fuzzy feelings, but they also are places where accidents happen. Safety experts say the kitchen is one of the most dangerous rooms in the home (the bathroom and garage rank up there, too). According to Meri-K Appy, president of the Home Safety Council (www .homesafetycouncil.org), a nonprofit group dedicated to preventing home injury, the majority of residential fires start in the kitchen—fire and burns are the third leading cause of unintentional injury in the home. Other potential hazards in the kitchen: falls (the number-one cause of home injury deaths), poisoning from toxic household products or medications (particularly worrisome if you have children), and cuts from sharp objects.

The essentials for making your kitchen safer are:

Fire-resistant oven mitts

An exhaust fan and good ventilation

Electrical appliances approved by UL or another third-party testing lab, and GFCI electrical outlets (located away from water sources)

Proper lighting (especially near food preparation areas)

Slip-resistant flooring (rugs or mats should be non-skid, with no curled edges) and a sturdy stepstool with nonslip treads

Antiscald devices on sink faucets

Child safety locks on all cabinets with cleaning products (opt for nontoxic products when possible)

Accessible emergency phone numbers

Overall Kitchen Safety Tips from the Experts

Fire-resistant oven mitts. Cooking is the cause of the majority of kitchen fires, and burns are the third most common cause of unintentional injury-related deaths in the home. Meri-K Appy says you should have proper hand and arm protection, especially when using substances like hot oil, which can be extremely dangerous. "If you're frying, protect exposed skin with an oven mitt, the kind that goes way up the arm," she says.

An exhaust fan and good ventilation. Cooking generates odors, steam, and fumes from smoke that can contribute to indoor pollution. Ventilation is particularly important if you cook with a gas stove, because a leak or malfunction can cause a buildup of carbon monoxide (CO), a colorless, odorless gas that can make you sick or, worse, kill you. (Other common sources of CO in the home are furnaces, space heaters, wood-burning stoves, and fireplaces.)

Electrical appliances approved by UL or another third-party lab, and GFCI electrical outlets. These should be located away from water sources. UL (Underwriters Laboratories) is an organization that sets public safety standards, and GFCI (ground fault circuit interrupter) outlets provide protection from shocks and electrical fires. "GFCIs should be installed anyplace where there is water and electricity," says Appy. "They prevent serious shock if electricity comes in contact with water." Also, unplug any appliances when not in use and secure cords so children can't pull them down.

Proper lighting. This is important especially near food preparation areas. Cuts (from using sharp objects like knives) and falls (from slippery surfaces) are common hazards in the kitchen. Be sure your kitchen has adequate lighting.

Slip-resistant flooring and a sturdy stepstool with nonslip treads. Rugs or mats should be nonskid, with no curled edges. Falls are the number-one cause of unintentional injury and death in the home. To avoid falls, keep kitchen floors clear of liquids or spilled food, make sure rugs or floor mats have nonskid backing (tack down edges that curl up), and use a sturdy stepstool to retrieve things from high shelves. "If you're remodeling or building a home, use slip-resistant flooring in the kitchen," Appy says.

Antiscald devices on sink faucets. According to the Consumer Product Safety Commission, scalding from extremely hot tap water is the cause of about 3,800 injuries each year. "I think scalding is underrecognized as a hazard," says Appy. "Hot water can be deadly, and typically people don't know what the temperature of their hot water is. The recommended safe temperature setting on your hot-water heater is 120 degrees." An antiscald device on a faucet will limit water flow if the temperature exceeds 120 degrees. (You may want to consult a plumber about installation.)

Child safety locks on all cabinets with cleaning products. Opt for nontoxic products when possible. "Read the labels on all household products," says Appy. "If you see the words 'Caution,' 'Warning,' 'Danger,' or 'Poison,' store the product out of sight and out of reach of children, in a cabinet with a child safety lock." Better yet, replace any toxic products with safer versions (for information on ingredients in clean-

ing products, check the National Library of Medicine (www
.householdproducts.nlm.nih.gov). For safer alternatives, try
brands like Seventh Generation, Greening the Cleaning,
Method, and BabyGanics. Or clean with household staples
like vinegar, baking soda, borax, lemon juice, salt, castile
soap, and washing soda. (And if you store medications in
the kitchen, keep them out of reach of children.)

Accessible emergency phone numbers. You have to think fast
in an emergency. Keep a contact list of important numbers
near the phone and be sure that everyone in the family (especially children) knows where it is. Numbers to keep handy:
fire department; police department; emergency medical services (it's 911 in most places in the United States, but check if
that's the case in your community); local poison control center (the national hotline is 800-222-1222); your family doctor;
your and your spouse's work numbers and cell phone numbers; your relatives', friends', and neighbors' numbers.

A word about fire extinguishers. Extinguishers can be an
adequate deterrent to many house fires, but they may not
be the right choice for the kitchen, especially if the fire is
from oil or grease. "Dry chemical extinguishers should not

be used on a pan fire," says Appy. "Instead, slide a pan lid or cookie sheet over the top of the pan." This removes the oxygen and smothers the fire. It must be done quickly, though, because a grease fire can spread very fast.

Still, it's advisable to keep an easy-to-operate fire extinguisher in your home, but take the time to educate yourself about how to use it. The problem is that you have to think fast in a fire. "The time to start reading directions is not when the fire has started," Appy says. In addition, the chemicals in extinguishers are released with strong force, which may create problems if the operator isn't prepared. "The extinguishing agent shoots out at very high pressure," she warns, "and the force of that agent can topple a pan and spread the fire, making things worse."

Not only should an extinguisher be easy to operate, Appy points out, but it should be the largest size you can handle. "With small extinguishers, the juice is gone in seconds, and if you don't do it right the first time, you may have made the situation worse and then squandered the limited window of opportunity you had to get to safety." You might consider getting a fire-extinguishing spray such as Tundra, made by First Alert (www.firstalerttundra.com). It's easy to operate and it fits on a counter.

Bathroom Essentials: What the Experts Say

In some ancient cultures bathing and grooming were elaborate, pleasurable rituals. For instance, for the average Roman a bath at the local thermae was a leisurely activity that would have taken an entire afternoon. It not only involved washing in hot and cold water but also being anointed with oils and perfumes, scraping the body with a utensil called a strigil, steaming, massaging, exercising, drinking wine, eating, socializing, and being entertained by jugglers or musicians.

Today most of us don't have as much time as the Romans did to luxuriate in bathing. But because we all live such hectic lives, the bathroom should be a place where we can relax and indulge ourselves. "The bathroom to me is a sanctuary," says Susie Coelho, the lifestyle expert and HGTV host. "It should feel like a room, not a bathroom, so I try to make it warm and bright and homey by adding carpeting, wooden furniture, and lots of decorative accessories. And if you have children, the bathroom is also a gathering place, where you're giving the kids a bath or washing their hair. So you should create practical places for people to sit down. Above all, it should feel comfortable."

Like the kitchen, the bathroom has become a showplace. Last year, Americans spent $70.2 billion remodeling their bathrooms, reports the National Kitchen and Bath Association.

Because we spend so much time there, the bathroom must not only be an attractive and comfortable place but also a functional and safe one. The essentials for the bathroom are:

Good-quality towels

A well-stocked medicine cabinet

Child safety locks on all cabinets with medications and personal care and cleaning products

Slip-resistant flooring (rugs or mats should be non-skid, with no curled edges)

Nonskid strips (or mat) in the tub or shower

Grab bars in the tub or shower

Nightlight and proper lighting

Antiscald devices in the tub and shower

Electrical devices approved by UL or another third-party testing lab, and GFCI electrical outlets (located away from water sources)

An exhaust fan and good ventilation

Overall Bathroom Tips from the Experts

Good-quality towels. When it comes to buying towels, appearance counts. "Brand is not that important, we found in our research," says Linda DeFranco, associate director of the product trend analysis department at Cotton Incorporated, a trade group for the cotton industry. "If the look and the softness are there, that's what consumers really want." Absorbency and durability also count. How do you know if a towel has those qualities? It helps to know what to look for. Here are some tips:

Types of towels. Most toweling in the United States is made of cotton. "Cotton absorbs moisture and releases it quickly so it dries faster," says DeFranco. Avoid cotton/poly blends. "You don't want blends, because water just rests on top of the fiber"—it is not absorbed, she says. The most common types of towels are terry cloth, which features uncut loops of yarn or "pile" on the surface of the fabric, and velour, which features shorter sheared loops on the surface of the fabric that give it a smooth, velvety sheen (velour tends to be less absorbent than terry cloth).

It's in the loop. Unlike bedsheets, towels do not list thread count. For towels with good absorbency, look for thick, tightly woven loops. In general, the thicker the loops on the surface of the fabric, the greater the absorbency, says DeFranco.

Types of cotton. Not all cotton is the same. Cotton is graded according to its staple (length). In general, the longer the staple, the finer (and costlier) the yarn. Higher-grade cotton used in toweling includes Egyptian cotton, grown on the Nile River and known for its luxurious feel and durability, and pima cotton (Supima is a trademark pima cotton), which is grown in the Southwest and has similar properties to Egyptian cotton. (For more information on cotton, see "Good-Quality Sheets," page 208.)

Laundering. With proper care, towels can last more than ten years. "Towels can last a long time, but be careful when washing," says DeFranco. Don't use extremely high temperatures, use a mild detergent (half the amount the manufacturer recommends, to ensure softness) and, above all, don't use bleach or fabric softener, she cautions. "People think they have to boil their towels and sheets—they don't. Very high temperatures make linens less durable," she says. "Bleach and fabric softener are really the worst things you can use on your linens because they eat away at the fiber and weaken it." Let towels dry before putting them in a hamper (they can get mildewed). Rotate your towels frequently. Interesting fact: The average American household, DeFranco says, has fifteen towels.

*A **well-stocked medicine cabinet.*** A medicine cabinet is a fixture in most bathrooms, but it's a bit of a misnomer, experts say. It's not a good idea to store medications in the bathroom, because constant heat and humidity can affect potency and cause deterioration. Medications should be kept in a cool, dry place, like a closet (away from children, of course). However, you should store a number of basic items in your medicine cabinet (see "Streamline Your Medicine Cabinet: The Essentials," page 223).

Child safety locks on all cabinets with medications and personal care and cleaning products. Opt for nontoxic varieties when possible. Keep all of these products out of the reach of children. Even a seemingly benign-looking product could pose a danger if you don't know what the ingredients are. "Consumers need to get in the habit of looking at labels before bringing products into their home," says Meri-K Appy, president of the Home Safety Council. "The words 'Caution,' 'Warning,' 'Danger,' and 'Poison' are signal for you to gather those products and lock them away using a child-safe lock. Those safety labels are there because some other family paid a terrible price."

To find out how safe the cleaning products you use are,

check the National Library of Medicine (www.household products.nlm.nih.gov). For cosmetics, check the Environmental Working Group (www.ewg.org), a nonprofit environmental watchdog organization, which has a database of more than 23,000 brand-name products. Each product is evaluated by its ingredients and given safety scores from 1 to 10.

Slip-resistant flooring (nonskid rugs or mats, with no curled edges), nonskid strips (or mat) in the tub or shower, grab bars in the tub or shower, and nightlight and proper lighting. All of these are preventive measures against falls, which, according to the Home Safety Council, are the number-one cause of unintentional injury and death in the home, accounting for about 5.1 million injuries and nearly 6,000 deaths a year. The bathroom is an especially accident-prone place because there are water sources and slippery surfaces like tile. Appy cautions, "Make sure there is no standing water on the floor."

Antiscald devices in tub and shower. "Hot water can be deadly, and typically people don't know what the temperature of their hot water is," says Appy. "The recommended safe temperature on your hot-water heater is 120 degrees, and a safe bathing temperature is 100 degrees." An antiscald device will limit water flow if the temperature exceeds 120 degrees. You may want to consult a plumber about installing such a device. Or you can replace your bathtub fixtures with a HotStop (h20tstop.com) hand shower, shower head, or tub spout. These products, which are easily installed, have built-in antiscald mechanisms.

Electrical appliances approved by UL or another third-party testing lab, and GFCI electrical outlets. Place these away from water sources. To ensure that your appliances are safe, buy only those devices with the UL (Underwriters Laboratories) seal. UL is an organization that sets public safety standards. Use extra caution with appliances like hair dryers, curling irons, shavers, and so on, in the bathroom. Keep clear of water sources. To avoid electric shock, have an electrician install GFCI (ground fault circuit interrupter) outlets, which prevent shock if electricity comes in contact with water and will shut off the current.

An exhaust fan and good ventilation. Without proper ventilation, the humid environment of the bathroom makes it the perfect breeding ground for mold, mildew, and bacteria. In addition, all that moisture can increase humidity levels in your home, damaging walls, paint, wallpaper, and building materials throughout your house.

Bedroom Essentials: What the Experts Say

Did you know that we spend about 222,000 hours of our lives asleep? According to sleep experts, your bed is the most utilized piece of furniture in your home. We all have stress in our lives and need a peaceful environment to unwind in. That's why it's imperative to create an oasis of calm in your bedroom.

How do you do that? "I prefer a bedroom to be neutral in color," says lifestyle expert Susie Coelho. "Mine is in shades of white, cream, and taupe, because I want it to feel serene. But it depends on what you want. If you want it to be more of a boudoir, then you might use deep rich reds and velvety fabrics."

Aside from being a beautiful, comfortable place, your bedroom should be safe. The essentials for the bedroom are:

A good-quality mattress (and bedspring)

A good-quality pillow (if you use one)

Good-quality sheets

A smoke alarm (in the bedroom and nearby hallway)

A carbon monoxide alarm (in or near the bedroom)

Nightlights (placed in passageways)

A working flashlight (in your night table)

Telephone next to your bed, with accessible emergency numbers

Overall Bedroom Tips from the Experts

A good-quality mattress and bedspring. The focal point of any bedroom is, of course, the bed—the most utilized piece of furniture in the home, experts say. Since we spend so much time in bed, our mattress should be the highest quality we can afford. These days there is a huge range of mattress choices. How do you know which is right for you?

"Mattresses are important, but there's very little research that's actually been done on them," says Dr. Scott D. Boden, an orthopedic surgeon, director of the Emory University Spine Center in Atlanta, and spokesman for the American Academy of Orthopedic Surgeons. "There's a lot of folklore and assumption."

One myth: the firmer the mattress the better.

"For the most part studies that have been done show that there is no best mattress firmness for everyone," says

Dr. Boden. "Medium-firm and medium are generally preferred by most people, but some people sleep better on a slightly softer one or a slightly harder one."

Experts say that when buying a mattress, the key word is comfort.

"It's really individual preference—whatever meets a person's needs in terms of comfort level," says Dr. Clete A. Kushida, director of the Stanford University Center for Human Sleep Research, and an officer on the board of directors for the American Academy of Sleep Medicine. Dr. Kushida stresses the importance of lying down on a mattress in the store to determine your comfort level. "There is such a wide selection of mattresses now, so you have to shop around carefully and test a mattress for as long as possible. The more exposure you have, the better you'll be prepared to know how you'll sleep."

Aside from comfort, what else should you look for? "A mattress should provide support but not to the point where it puts a person's body out of alignment or causes tissue strain," says Dr. Kushida. For example, he says, "Spine specialists tend to recommend that one of the better postures to sleep is on your side with hips and knees slightly flexed. But if you sleep on your side and your mattress is too firm, it's going to be uncomfortable because it's going to put pressure on the shoulders and the hips."

On the other hand, says Dr. Boden, a mattress that's too soft may contribute to back problems. "If you don't have a supportive mattress, your back sort of flattens out. Like the arch of your foot, your back is arched in places, so when you sleep you want it to rest in that natural position. A mattress that's too soft may put your back in a less than ideal position when resting, which could load certain joints or stretch certain muscles or tendons, which puts stress on the back."

A good mattress matters more as we age. "A mattress becomes more important as we get older because we get more chronic pain syndromes, like back pain, neck pain, chronic insomnia, and sleep disorders," says Dr. Kushida. "Basically, if you're a child, an adolescent, or a young adult, you can sleep on almost any surface."

Another reason for investing in a good mattress is that it will keep its shape better and last longer. A quality mattress should last five to seven years (some experts say even ten years), depending on usage. To keep it clean, use a mattress pad—it protects the mattress and creates a barrier against dust mites, especially important if you suffer from allergies. For more protection, consider using a dust-mite-resistant mattress encasing in addition to a mattress pad. To clean a mattress, use a vacuum cleaner. Also, rotate the mattress every few weeks to cut down on wear and tear.

A good-quality pillow. Like a mattress, a pillow is a matter of personal comfort. The most important thing is that it provides enough support for the proper alignment of your head, neck, and spine. If your pillow doesn't do that, you can wake up with a stiff neck or an aching back. How much elevation you need is determined by your body type and what position you sleep in. For instance, most people sleep on their side. "How broad your shoulders are will determine how elevated your pillow should be," says Dr. Boden. "If the pillow is too low it will flex your neck and kink it in a downward direction, and if it's too high it will flex your neck and kink it in the other direction."

These days many manufacturers offer specific pillows designed for various sleeping positions: In general, firmer pillows are recommended for side sleepers, medium pillows for back sleepers, and soft for stomach sleepers (note that sleeping on the stomach can put stress on the neck and back). But there are no hard and fast rules about firmness—it's whatever is most comfortable for you. Common fillers are down, feathers, latex foam, hypoallergenic down substitutes, and specialty pillows made of hemp, buckwheat, and organic cotton, wool, or silk. Prices run the gamut, so buy the best one you can afford.

Pillows should be replaced every few years, depending on quality and the type of materials. For instance, a good down pillow can last ten years. How do you know if you need a new pillow? If it's flattened out and not giving you support or if it smells or is badly stained, it's time for a new one. To test firmness, fold the pillow over; if it doesn't bounce back, it's probably worn out.

Keep pillows clean, especially if you have allergies. Over time they can be a haven for dust mites, mold, and mildew. Wash pillows on a regular basis, according to the manufacturer's recommendations. To reduce allergens, use dust-mite-resistant pillow slips.

Good-quality sheets. When it comes to buying sheets, a little knowledge goes a long way. There are a lot of choices out there, but fancy price tags and designer labels don't necessarily mean the quality is higher than lower-profile brands. Most sheets on the market are 100 percent cotton or cotton/polyester blends. For sheets, all cotton is preferable because it is more absorbent than cotton/poly. When choosing sheets, here is what you should consider:

Thread count. "Thread count is the number of threads per square inch lengthwise and widthwise—the warp and the weft—of the fabric," says Linda DeFranco, associate director of the product trend analysis department at Cotton Incorporated, a trade group for the cotton industry. Thread count in most sheets generally falls within the 180 to 500 range. But, she says, the numbers don't always tell the story. "People think that the higher the thread count, the better the quality, but it's not necessarily so. It's a bit deceiving. With thread count you have to look at a few different factors, one of them being the ply of the yarn. You can have single-ply yarn, which is just one yarn, or you can have double-ply yarn, which is two yarns twisted together to make one yarn."

This is where it gets tricky. Manufacturers can claim a higher thread count by using double-ply yarns. "Technically you can have a 600-thread-count sheet but it could really be a 300-thread-count sheet because they're using double-ply yarns," says DeFranco.

So if you're buying a 600-thread-count sheet, make sure it's 600-single-ply threads you're getting.

Not that there's anything wrong with double ply. DeFranco says that double-ply can be stronger than single ply, but it also can be heavier. "Double ply has more durability and probably will last longer," she says.

Types of weave. Sheets are available in four types of weave. Percale is a closely woven plain weave. "It's the finest available and will give you the highest thread count," says DeFranco. "It has a fluid, almost silk-like feel." Flannel is a softer medium-weight plain weave with a raised, soft surface. "It has a fluffy, supple feel and it's warm for the winter months," she says. Jersey is a pliable fabric knitted on a circular, warped-knit or flatbed machine, and sateen is a weave with a smooth, lustrous surface and very soft feel.

Quality and types of cotton. The quality of the yarn is another factor to consider. Cotton is graded according to its staple (length). In general, the longer the staple, the finer the yarn. The following are the most common types of cotton used in sheeting. Upland cotton has a medium staple (this can vary depending on the fineness of the yarn). "Most sheets in the United States are made with Upland cotton," says DeFranco. Egyptian cotton has a very long staple. Grown on the banks of the Nile, Egyptian cotton is known for its silky, luxurious feel and durability. "It is more expensive because there are limited quantities, and it's a finer yarn, so you can fit more threads per square inch," says DeFranco. Pima cotton has a long staple. Grown in the Southwest, pima cotton (Supima is the trademark for pima) is a hybrid of Upland and Egyptian cotton and is also known for softness and durability. But, says DeFranco, you can get those qualities in Upland cotton, too. "It really depends on how fine the yarn is."

It's all in the hand. What matters most to consumers when they buy sheets? "Based on our research, the most important things are softness, durability, price, and then color," she says. "I always recommend feeling the sheets before you buy them to see what the hand is." How a fabric is treated is another consideration. "The way a sheet is finished can affect the hand, so you really have to touch them to see if they have the softness, the luster, and the look you want in your bedroom."

Laundering. Linens can last for many years if cared for properly. "My mother-in-law has had some sheets for thirty years," says DeFranco. When washing sheets, she says, don't use extremely high temperatures and *never* use bleach or fabric softener. "They eat away at the fiber and makes it less durable over time." Also, don't overdry linens.

If you collect antique white linens, they need special care, says Susie Coelho. Vintage linens can get yellowed. One simple way to whiten them is to use Biz, which whitens without bleach. "Biz is great—all the people who sell vintage linens use it," she says. "Don't use bleach on old linens—it's too strong, it will wear the fibers down, and you'll get holes." And don't put vintage linens in the dryer, she warns. "Hang them to dry, and iron them on gentle or steam them. When you iron them, put a light cotton fabric on top so that the iron doesn't leave marks."

A smoke alarm (in the bedroom and nearby hallway). Smoke alarms save lives. According to the National Fire Protection Association, 65 percent of reported home fire deaths occur in residences with no alarms or no working alarms. Another fact: The majority of home fire deaths occur at night. So fire prevention is especially critical near all bedrooms. Place a UL-approved smoke alarm in your bedroom and in a nearby hallway. "At a minimum you need one smoke alarm on every level of your home and in or near every sleeping area," says Meri-K Appy of the Home Safety Council.

She recommends an interconnected alarm system, which sets off alarms in all locations of the home regardless of where the fire is. "Let's say the fire is downstairs and you have a single-station alarm near it and you have a single-station alarm in your bedroom," she says. "The alarm closest to the fire will detect smoke, but you may be too far away to hear it, or you may not hear it immediately. With alarms that are interconnected, when the first alarm sounds they all do." This gives you and your family more time to escape if the fire has started in another part of your home. Hard-wired, interconnected alarms should be installed by an electrician and should also have backup batteries. You can also get wireless interconnected smoke alarm systems. The fire and security company Kidde is offering the first UL-approved system—for information, go to www.kidde wireless.com.

A carbon monoxide alarm (in or near the bedroom). Carbon monoxide (CO) is a colorless, odorless, and very toxic gas that can be fatal—in fact, it's called the silent killer. CO is a gas produced from any fuel-burning apparatus—normally in very small amounts that dissipate into the air. But when fuel is not vented properly (if there is an obstruction or malfunction, for instance), dangerous levels of CO can build up and turn deadly. Common sources of CO in the home are furnaces, space heaters, wood-burning stoves, fireplaces (if a chimney is blocked), gas stoves, idling cars, or lawn mowers powered up in a garage or enclosed area. So it's crucial to keep all appliances in working order and to make sure your home has good ventilation with lots of fresh air. Place a UL-approved carbon monoxide alarm in a central place (like a hallway) near all bedrooms.

Nightlights (placed in passageways). Other potential bedroom problems: slips and falls—which are the number one cause of unintentional injury and death in the home (especially among older people and children). Keep a nightlight in passageways should you have to get up in the middle of the night. Also make sure area rugs and throw rugs are tacked down securely, and don't place them in passageways where you might trip on the edges.

*A **working flashlight.*** This is a no-brainer. Always keep a flashlight (with fresh or rechargeable batteries) in your night table. You never know when you may need it.

{general safety tips for every home}

• Be cautious when using candles in your home, especially in the bedroom. Never leave them unattended anywhere. The National Fire Protection Association says that in 2004 about 17,200 reported home fires were started by candles, and 38 percent of candle fires started in the bedroom. "We recommend not using them in the bedroom because it's too easy to fall asleep and forget them," says Meri-K Appy, president of the Home Safety Council. "Never trust a lit candle to behave itself." New battery-operated candles offer a safe alternative.

• Don't smoke in your bedroom (for the same reason you shouldn't use candles—it's too easy to fall asleep with a lit cigarette). Better yet, don't smoke in your home at all. "If there are smokers in the home, consider an outdoor smoking area," says Appy.

• Install a fire sprinkler system in your home if you are remodeling or building a new home. "A fire sprinkler system gives you the best possible protection from fire," says Appy. "If there is a fire, water is automatically sprayed on the flames. The sprinkler system keeps the fire small or puts it out."

• Install smoke and carbon monoxide alarms on every level of your home.

• Keep an easy-to-operate fire extinguisher on each floor and be trained to use it. See "A Word About Fire Extinguishers" on page 194.

• Prepare a fire escape plan and conduct regular drills with your family.

• Get a fire escape ladder if your bedroom is on the second or third floor.

• Use appliances approved by a third-party testing lab such as UL and install GFCI electrical outlets in rooms with water sources (bathroom, kitchen, laundry room, pool area).

• Have an emergency supply kit (see "How Prepared Are You for an Emergency?"on opposite page).

- Keep working flashlights in accessible places.
- Get a good home alarm system installed. ⬚

{how prepared are you for an emergency?}

We live in uncertain times. Safety experts say every home should have an emergency supply kit. According to Ready America (www.ready.gov), a division of the U.S. Department of Homeland Security, items to include are:

- Water—one gallon of water per person per day for at least three days, for drinking and sanitation

- Food—at least a three-day supply of nonperishable food

- Battery-powered or hand-crank radio and a NOAA weather radio with tone alert, and extra batteries for both

- Flashlight and extra batteries

- First-aid kit

- Whistle, to signal for help

- Dust mask, to help filter contaminated air and plastic sheeting and duct tape to shelter-in-place

- Moist towelettes, garbage bags, and plastic ties for personal sanitation

- Wrench or pliers to turn off utilities

- Can opener for food (if kit contains canned food)

- Local maps

For information on preparedness for specific emergencies, see Ready America (www.ready.gov), the American Red Cross (www.redcross.org), the Centers for Disease Control and Prevention (www.bt.cdc.gov), the Federal Alliance for Safe Homes (www.flash.org), and the Federal Emergency Management Agency (www.fema.gov). ☑

{food prep basics}

To protect yourself from food-borne illnesses, follow these simple precautions:

1. Wash your hands with soap and water before preparing food. Avoid preparing food for others if you have a diarrheal illness. And don't change a baby's diaper when preparing food—it can spread illness.

2. Cook meat, poultry, and eggs thoroughly. Ground beef should be cooked to an internal temperature of 160°F (use a meat thermometer). Eggs should be cooked until the yolk is firm.

3. Don't cross-contaminate one food with another. Wash hands, utensils, and cutting boards after they have been in contact with raw meat or poultry and before they touch another food. Put cooked meat on a clean platter—don't put it back on the one that held raw meat.

4. Refrigerate leftovers promptly. Bacteria can grow quickly at room temperature, so chill leftover foods if they are not going to be eaten within four hours. Large amounts of food will cool more quickly if they are divided into several shallow containers for refrigeration.

5. Rinse fresh fruits and vegetables in running tap water to remove visible dirt and grime. Discard the outermost leaves of a head of lettuce or cabbage. Because bacteria can grow on the cut surface of fruits and vegetables, be careful not to contaminate these foods while slicing them up on the cutting board, and avoid leaving cut produce at room temperature for many hours.

6. Report suspected food-borne illnesses to your local public health department. ☑

Source: Adapted from "Foodborne Illness," a document from the Division of Bacterial and Mycotic Diseases at the Centers for Disease Control and Prevention

{more kitchen safety tips}

Want to reduce the risk of accidents in your kitchen? Meri-K Appy of the Home Safety Council offers the following tips:

1. Never leave the stove unattended when cooking. "The most common cause of cooking fires is that someone walked away from the stove or turned their back to answer the phone or whatever," she says. "This is of particular concern when frying food with hot oil. Supervision is key."

2. Never wear loose clothing when cooking. "Some people get lackadaisical—they'll cook in a big chenille bathrobe," she says. "Remember, you're near a heat source and a hot surface and you're wearing something combustible. Make sure your sleeves are tight fitting or short or you've rolled them up."

3. To contain a pan fire, especially when frying with hot oil or cooking at high temperatures, keep a cookie sheet or pot lid and oven mitt handy. "If your cooking catches fire in the pan, you can immediately grab the cookie sheet or the lid and put

it right over the pan," she says. "That will remove the oxygen and smother the fire. But it has to be done instantly because a pan fire with oil can create a very large flame. And if you have items like dish towels, draperies, or a window nearby, that fire can spread very fast. The minute it does that it's already too late to think about putting it out yourself." Also, keep the stovetop and oven clean and free of grease and food. A buildup of substances could catch fire or add to the spread of an existing fire, she says. Always keep paper products, dish towels, and any flammable materials far away from the stove.

4. To treat burns, immediately immerse the affected area in tepid to cool—not icy—water for at least three minutes or longer. "Every second you delay, that heat is boring down in the layers of the skin and it won't stop doing that until it cools, so you really have to act instantly," says Appy. "The cool-a-burn technique works for pretty much any burn. If you suspect a serious burn, keep it cool and call for emergency help."

5. Use caution with sharp objects like knives or mandolines (and store them out of a child's reach).

When using a cutting board, make sure the board sits securely on the counter (put a wet towel underneath it), and cut with the blade away from your body. Wash big knives by hand; don't put them in the dishwasher. ⬀

{streamline your medicine cabinet: the essentials}

What's one of the biggest clutter zones in your house? The medicine cabinet, says Dr. Rick Kellerman, president of the American Academy of Family Physicians. "People have too much stuff—especially too many medications that are old and expired." Get rid of them, he says, because they won't do you any good. A medication that's expired may not be effective—and could even be unsafe because of chemical changes.

"Over time some medications change," he says. "For instance, certain medications are affected by heat and light. Or if it's a liquid solution, it may become more concentrated than what it was initially." Heed expiration dates. "Do a spring cleaning every year, in terms of what's expired, or if you have any prescription medications that you no longer take— like antibiotics you didn't finish, or old medications your doctor switched you from. Throw those old medications away."

Keep it simple, Dr. Kellerman says. Buy over-the-counter medications only when you need them. For instance, if you rarely have indigestion, don't buy an antacid just to have it. "If you have problems with stomach upset, and you've been properly evaluated by your physician, then buy it. But to go out and buy it because you might need it in a year is just a waste of money."

Also, you don't need to buy antiseptics to clean routine cuts and scrapes. "Soap and water are still the best antiseptic," he says.

Dr. Kellerman lists these essentials for your medicine cabinet:

Medical gloves (to wear while treating wounds, to avoid spreading infection)

Adhesive bandages (for minor cuts)

Telfa pads (for wounds)

Gauze pads (for wounds)

Adhesive tape

Tweezers

A thermometer (the best one you can afford)

Calibrated measuring spoon (more than one if you have children)

Acetaminophen (for fever, aches and pains, and arthritis)

Ibuprofen (for fever, aches and pains, muscle strain)

Aspirin (for prevention of arthritis and heart disease; discuss with your physician; do not give to young children, because of the risk of Reye's syndrome)

Antacid (optional; if history of indigestion)

Antihistamine (optional; if history of allergies)

EpiPen (epinephrine; optional; if history of allergies or asthma)

Calamine lotion (for insect bites)

Things you don't need: Disinfectants (soap and water are best); antibiotic ointments (Dr. Kellerman doesn't recommend them: "Some people can have allergic reactions, and I don't know that they really help in terms of healing"); decongestants ("Buy them only that time of season when you need them"); hydrocortisone cream ("Not usually necessary—use calamine lotion for insect bites"); syrup of ipecac ("Twenty or twenty-five years ago it was standard for poisoning, but the thinking has changed—there have been questions about its effectiveness").

Other things you need: A current list of all medications you are taking. "This includes not only prescription drugs but any over-the-counter or herbal medications," he says. "Keep it with you because if you have to go to a new doctor or to the emergency room, you might not remember what you're taking, and doctors have to know because of drug interactions."

Storage: Where should you keep meds? Actually, the bathroom is not the best place, says Dr. Kellerman (as well as the FDA), because the extremes of heat and humidity may affect potency and cause deterioration. "Keep medications in a place that's more temperature- and humidity-controlled," he says. A cool, dry place like a linen closet is good— out of the reach of children, of course.

First–aid kit: Dr. Kellerman suggests creating a mobile first-aid kit for your car (especially for road trips). In addition to the above list, he recommends packing: a blanket; a clean, dry towel, to apply pressure if someone has a cut or wound; bottled water, for cleaning cuts or wounds; and an alcohol-based hand sanitizer, such as Purell. The main thing, he says, is to have "everything organized and in one place when you need it." ☙

{design 101:
the art of "undecoration"}

In the world of interior design, Mario Buatta is royalty. Fondly known for decades as the "prince of chintz" because of his love of that floral fabric, the New York designer has an international reputation for creating rooms that look not only sublimely beautiful but also "undecorated," meaning comfortable and lived in. Named by *Architectural Digest* as one of the Design 100 and by *Town & Country* as among the top twelve designers in the United States, Buatta has worked for a notable list of clients—Mariah Carey, Barbara Walters, and Henry Ford II, to name just a few. Among his many projects are Blair House, the official guest quarters of the White House; and the Henry Francis du Pont Winterthur Museum galleries in Delaware.

What are the essentials to a well-designed room? Mario Buatta offers his views on the basics:

Architectural changes. If you can improve a room with structural changes, it can make a huge difference.

"Whether it's changing the windows or the mantel or the opening to the room—how you enter and how you leave—it's important to get the architecture right," he says. "Of course, it's a lot easier to make these changes in a house than in an apartment."

A floor plan. Create a workable floor plan to help you determine where things will be placed. "Think about seating arrangements first, then add tables and other pieces of furniture," he says. "This really helps you to see what the room is going to look like."

Color. Decide on the color scheme you want in the room and consider how it fits in with the rest of the home. "Think about what color the room will be, and the colors of the rest of the house or apartment," Buatta says. "The colors should be pleasing as soon as you enter. And they should be pleasing when you walk from room to room—nothing should be jarring." On the other hand, "there are no rules about color—it's what's pleasing to you."

Fabrics. Buy the best fabrics you can afford. Color, pattern, and longevity are key considerations.

"Think about what's suitable for the room," Buatta says. "I try to make things cozy and comfortable and colorful. I use a lot of patterns in a room, so they all look like they landed at different times." Comfort and quality are also important. "You sleep in a bed for eight hours a day, but your chairs and sofas should be just as comfortable as your bed. And they should be of good quality, because you're going to have them a long time. I've had my sofa for thirty-one years, and it's still great. The longer I have it, the more comfortable it seems to get."

Composition and balance. Consider the overall aesthetics of the room. "Think of the room as if you were an artist painting a canvas," Buatta advises. "You want a pleasing composition and a balance of color, so that you don't see four red things in one corner and four green things in another corner."

Scale. Think about your furniture and its relationship to the room. One of the most common mistakes people make is in misjudging scale—how furniture fits into a big or small room. "People buy sofas that are too small, chairs that are too small, cabinets that are too small—

they often don't understand size, and what furniture is going to look like in a room," Buatta says. Scale can be deceiving: In a small room, for example, a big canopy bed can actually make the room look bigger, he says. And in a big room, smaller furniture can look like pieces of a puzzle scattered all over.

The element of surprise: Mix things up—don't strive for perfection. Buatta compares rooms to gardens. "They continue to grow—they are never really finished. They evolve over a lifetime." And it's fine to mix periods, he says. "I mix everything—it makes the house come together. I don't believe that everything has to be an antique—you can mix old and new. If you have a room that's all one period, it's boring."

For the budget-conscious. You can make design improvements without breaking the bank. Even a simple coat of paint can make a big difference. Or a change of slipcovers. "I had a client who had four sets of slipcovers," Buatta says, "one for every season. It changed the whole look of the room. Some people change the objects on their tables from season to season. You can also change pillows and throws. And you can do a lot with sheets. You can use them for slipcovers and a lot of other things."

Things to avoid. Don't buy impulsively, especially big-ticket items. "Wait until the right thing comes along," Buatta advises. "Don't think, 'I'll buy this for now.' What you're buying is an investment, and if you buy a bad investment, you have to live with it." ⏃

{bedroom allergen control}

Is your sleep being compromised by bad air in your bedroom? For allergy and asthma sufferers, the bedroom can be a minefield of potential problems—from dust mites to pet dander to mold. Here are some ways to clear the air and catch some restful Z's:

• Keep pets out of your bedroom and away from pillows and bedding.

• Change sheets at least once a week (twice if you perspire a lot) and wash them in hot water.

• Place dust-mite-resistant covers over your pillows and mattress.

• Buy hypoallergenic or organic bedding made of natural materials like cotton, silk, wool, or hemp. High-quality natural bedding products are available on many websites, including www.allergybuyers club.com, www.coyuchi.com, www.gaiam.com, www .cuddledown.com, www.furnature.com, www.lands end.com, www.dreamsoftbedware.com, www.life kind.com, www.greensage.com, www.thecompany store.com, and www.earthfriendlygoods.com.

• Consider getting a Hepa filter or air purifier.

• Keep your bedroom clean and dust free; use a Hepa vacuum regularly.

• Keep your bedroom well ventilated with fresh air. ☂

{the next big thing: small homes}

Living large is not an essential. Today there is a growing movement toward smaller eco-friendlier homes—to save resources and money, among other reasons. Many builders and designers around the country are offering small, affordable, practical, and beautiful houses (some prefab) that have just about everything you need.

The New York Times and other publications have featured articles about companies including the Tumbleweed Tiny House Company (www.tumble weedhouses.com), Alchemy Architects (www .weehouses.com), Modern Cabana (www.modern cabana.com), the Cottage Company (www.cottage company.com), and Cusato Cottages (www.cusato cottages.com). Cusato designed the Katrina Cottage for victims of the hurricane, and the model is now available at Lowe's (www.lowes .com).

For more information, go to the website of the Small House Society (www.smallhouse

society.com), which promotes small houses, and The Not So Big House (www.notsobighouse.com), a site started by the architect Sarah Susanka, author of *The Not So Big Life: Making Room for What Really Matters* and *The Not So Big House: A Blueprint for the Way We Really Live.* ⬀

{it's easy to be green}

Not everyone can afford to install solar panels, but you don't have to make major changes to be eco-friendly. Doug Moss, publisher and cofounder of *E/The Environmental Magazine* and coeditor of the book *Green Living: The E Magazine Handbook for Living Lightly on the Earth,* says there are many small ways you can save energy, reduce waste, and make your home healthier. Here's how:

• Replace incandescent bulbs with energy-efficient compact fluorescent lightbulbs (CFLs). They last about ten times longer and use 75 percent less energy than incandescents. "We put them in our house eight years ago and I swear that it's only fairly recently that I've started replacing them," says Moss. (Note: CFLs contain mercury; for information on disposal, go to www.energystar.gov; click on "Lighting.")

• Be certain that all appliances (like dishwashers, refrigerators, and washing machines) have the EPA's Energy Star symbol.

• Install low-flow showerheads and low-flush toilets to conserve water. The U.S. Geological Survey estimates that the average American uses about 80 to 100 gallons of water a day—much of it for flushing toilets and taking showers and baths.

• Replace toxic cleaning products and cosmetics with eco-friendlier versions. Check out the products you use at the National Library of Medicine (www .householdproducts.nlm.nih.gov) and the Environmental Working Group (www.ewg.com). For safer cleaning alternatives, try brands like Seventh

Generation, Greening the Cleaning, Method, and BabyGanics. Or clean the old-fashioned way with household staples like white vinegar, baking soda, borax, lemon juice, salt, castile soap, and washing soda.

• Use low-VOC paint in your home. VOCs (volatile organic compounds) are low-level chemical emissions from many household products (including paints and lacquers, paint strippers, cleaning supplies, pesticides, building materials, and furnishings), which contribute to indoor air pollution. For "greener" paints and finishes, check out companies like AFM (www.afmsafecoat.com) and BioShield (www.bioshieldpaint.com). "Even some mainstream companies like Benjamin Moore now offer them," Doug Moss says.

• Compost your biodegradable food if you can (this may not be practical in a small city apartment).

• Buy locally produced food. There are many reasons for supporting local agriculture, among them: Products are fresher because they were picked recently and probably are more nutritious than something that was picked weeks before and shipped, and it cuts down on the use of fossil fuels, which are required to ship products to destinations sometimes thousands of miles away. "What's the point of eating something organic if it's shipped from halfway around the world?" says Moss.

• Eat safe seafood. "It's not just the mercury issue—it's the whole idea of depleting the fisheries," says Moss. For information on what seafood to eat, check www.epa.gov/waterscience/fish, www.audubon.org (click on "Audubon at Home"), www.oceansalive .org, and www.blueocean.org/seafood.

• Don't buy so much stuff. Buy only what you need, and when you can, buy items that can be recycled. By living more simply, we not only reduce waste in our community, but we also decrease the potential for clutter in our homes.

• Use tap water. It is estimated that Americans consume about 30 billion single-serving plastic bottles of water a year. The problems: Most of the empties are not recycled, and it takes millions of barrels of oil to produce all those bottles, contributing to global warming. And why buy water when it's free from your tap? "I ride a bike to work and I'm appalled by the number of plastic bottles I see tossed on the road," says Moss. "The average person is under the false impression that there's something wrong with the tap water. I'd say that for the most part municipal water is very safe—unless you're living in an area where factory emissions are coming in your backyard."

• Keep your home ventilated with fresh air. The EPA says the air in your home (chemical vapors given off from carpeting, furnishings, paints, household cleaners, and building materials—as well as allergens generated from mold or dust) can be about 100 times more toxic than outdoor air. "This is another one of those no-brainer kind of things, whether it's an environmental issue or not, fresh air in the home is better than not," says Moss. "Most environmental issues are really about health, not about tree hugging."

• Use a manual lawn mower instead of a gas-powered mower. "Those little engines are quite polluting," says Moss. "They waste a lot of fuel because they burn a mixture of gas and oil."

• Buy eco-friendly home furnishings and building materials, made from all-natural sustainable materials, without using toxic chemicals. Check out companies like Furnature (www.furnature.com) and EcoTimber (www.ecotimber.com) or websites that sell "green" furniture, such as www.earthfriendly goods.com and greensage.com.

• Reuse plastic shopping bags. According to some estimates, it takes about 12 million barrels of oil to produce the billions of plastic bags we use annually (only 1 percent are actually recycled, according to the EPA). To cut back on accumulating plastic bags, use a canvas tote bag to carry groceries and other purchases.

• For information on all things environmental, check *E/The Environmental Magazine* (emagazine.com), the Environmental Protection Agency (www.epa.gov), and the American Council for an Energy-Efficient

Economy (aceee.org). (Are you an ecofashionista? To find out more, see "On the Outside: Clothing," page 125.) 🔗

{the art of letting go: decluttering}

Is your bedroom, basement, garage, or attic jammed with the detritus of modern life—from old computer monitors to stacks of Grandma's *National Geographics* that you can't bear to part with? If more and more stuff is taking over your home like kudzu, you're not alone.

Clutter is a constant battle for most Americans, says professional organizer Peter Walsh of the show *Clean Sweep* on TLC, author of *It's All Too Much: An Easy Plan for Living a Richer Life with Less Stuff*.

The four most problematic areas, he says, are "paperwork, which people struggle with all the time; clothing, especially the closet in the master bedroom; the garage, or what I call the black hole of clutter; and kids' toys."

Why do we hang on to so much stuff? "It's overwhelmingly one of two things: fear or control," Walsh says. "They are the two overarching factors, and they evidence themselves in two types of things people can't let go of. The first is what I call memory clutter, and that's the stuff that reminds us of an important person, event, or occasion in the past. The fear is if I let go of the object, I'll lose the memory. The second type is 'I might need it one day' clutter. And that's the stuff you hold on to in preparing for a whole lot of possible futures that you imagine in your head. And that's largely about insecurity or a need to control one's destiny."

When should you be concerned? "In moderate forms, there's nothing wrong with holding on to stuff that reminds you of something important in the past and it's appropriate to plan for the future," he says. "It's when those things take over your space that it's a problem."

How do you get a handle on it all? "I tackle it from a different perspective," he says. "For me, and

I'm absolutely convinced of this, if you focus on the stuff, you will *never* get organized. *Never.* The stuff is a distraction. The very first step in decluttering is to ask yourself, 'What is the vision for the life I want?' From there you decide, 'What is my goal and what is my dream for my home, and for each room?' That's the stepping-off point. Once you have that vision, that goal, that dream clearly in mind, then you start looking at the stuff and say, 'Does this item help me achieve that vision?' If it does, hold on to it. And if it doesn't, what's it doing in your space?"

He says that asking yourself these questions removes any pangs of guilt you might feel. "This takes all the discussion away from 'I paid good money for this' or 'I inherited this.' "

In the end, he says, you have to respect the limits of the space you have. "It's about quality of life, not quantity of stuff." (For information on decluttering your closets and paring down your wardrobe, see "On the Outside: Clothing," page 125.) ⬀

II. THE KEY TO THE KINGDOM: A HEALTHY MIND

Nothing is good or bad but

thinking makes it so.

—WILLIAM SHAKESPEARE

*T*he health of the mind is as critical to our survival as is the health of the body. What goes on in our heads—thoughts, feelings, attitudes, moods—can have the power to heal us or harm us.

What determines a healthy mind? It's a complex question. Each one of us is a product of our biology (genetics and brain chemistry), our environment, and our experiences. Though we all have our share of problems, worries, disappointments, and painful events—you can't get through life without them—it is how we cope with these stresses and ups and downs that is one of the critical factors in maintaining mind health.

While the majority of people certainly are not mentally ill, the simple fact is that some of us function a lot better in the world than others. There are certain essential characteristics that healthy-minded people share, and they are identified by several of the country's leading mental health experts in the following pages.

The essentials for a healthy mind are:

Love and connection

A sense of control

Mindfulness and acceptance

The ability to be real

Physical and mental exercise

Reaching Out: Love and Connection

Shared joy is a double joy; shared sorrow is half a sorrow.

—SWEDISH PROVERB

The need to love and be loved is fundamental to being human—it's part of our genetic makeup. In fact, the latest research in neuroscience suggests that the circuitry in our brains is programmed for social connection. Sharing and caring are good for our mental and physical wellness. Studies show that people who have strong social networks are happier and healthier than those who feel isolated and lonely. They experience less stress and even live longer—research says that married people live about five years longer than single or widowed people. The essentials for love and connection are:

The ability to form close bonds with others

The capacity to give and receive emotional support

Why We Need Love and Connection

The need to connect with others is embedded in the hardware in our brains. Within days of birth, infants make eye contact and seem able to read facial expressions. We also appear to have an innate concern for others. It is well documented that when infants hear the sound of other babies crying, they respond with tears. Interestingly, recent studies show that when babies hear a tape of their own crying, they do not respond—it is only when they hear the cries of other babies. This need to communicate with and identify with others—the awareness of something outside of ourselves—is what makes us human and grounds us in reality. As the novelist Iris Murdoch said, "Love is the difficult realization that something other than oneself is real."

"We are wired as social creatures—we need each other. It is essential for a healthy mind and a healthy body," says Joan Borysenko, Ph.D., a psychologist and author of *Your Soul's Compass: What Is Spiritual Guidance?* and *Minding the Body, Mending the Mind*. "When human beings get in isolation we know they get more anxious and more depressed. Our thoughts turn into themselves and that's not good."

Evidence shows that loneliness weakens the immune system. People who feel isolated are more likely to suffer from higher levels of stress, which produces the damaging hormone cortisol. Lonely people also are at risk for developing depression, anxiety, alcoholism, and other addictive behaviors. Without other people to share experiences, life can feel empty and hopeless. It is through relationships—with our partners, our family, our friends, and our community—that we get to know ourselves.

Unfortunately, isolation is a problem of modern-day life, and some studies suggest that our social circles are shrinking. While we need the support of our family, we also need outside friendships. These days many of us are getting by without a little help from our friends. A 2006 study from Duke University and the University of Arizona found that Americans have fewer close friends today than they had two decades ago. In fact, 25 percent of survey participants said they had no close friends at all to confide in. Researchers believe that our social circles are dwindling because of the increased amount of time people spend working and the rise in Internet communication.

Essentials: What the Experts Say

Love and connection are as fundamental as eating and sleeping. The essential components are:

The ability to form close bonds with others. All healthy human beings have a need for intimacy—to feel close to others, to feel understood, and to feel a sense of belonging. It is one of the foundations of a healthy mind, experts say. "Love and connection are the most important things," says David H. Barlow, Ph.D., a professor of psychology and psychiatry and director of the Center for Anxiety and Related Disorders at Boston University. "The field of positive psychology has shown in study after study after study that the greatest predictor of well-being and happiness is social embeddedness and the close connections you have with family, friends, and community," observes Dr. Barlow, a pioneer in the field of clinical psychology and the author of more than five hundred research articles.

Connectedness has a powerful effect on our mind and our body. When we have loving feelings, our brains produce a feel-good hormone called oxytocin, which decreases stress hormone levels, improves mood, lowers blood pressure, and may even affect how fast we heal, among other things. Oxytocin is produced in the hypothalamus, the part of the brain associated with pleasure.

"We have a fundamental need to be loved," says Dr. Borysenko. "The Greeks had a word for it, *thymos*, which is the need for recognition, the need to be seen. And they believed it was the strongest need there was—that wars were fought over it."

The capacity to give and receive emotional support. Being with people who understand us and accept us makes us feel we are not alone in the world, that we can cope with all the stresses life brings us. It inspires trust and confidence, making us feel more comfortable in sharing our thoughts and feelings—the good things as well as problems and doubts—without concerns about being criticized or judged.

"It's having a sense of support, the old folk wisdom that shared grief is divided and shared joy is multiplied—that kind of thing sums it up well, I think," says Dr. Barlow.

Emotional support is something we need throughout our lives. "We need people in our lives with a generous spirit who can help us work through life's challenges," says Dr. Michael Craig Miller, a psychiatrist, editor in chief of the *Harvard Mental Health Letter,* and assistant professor of psychiatry at Harvard Medical School. "Your development doesn't stop at age five or age twelve or age eighteen. We grow and develop throughout life and we need people. It's very difficult to do alone. We need people who can help us tolerate our own turmoil, people who we feel love us despite ourselves."

We also need to be there for others. "Not only do we need to be receptive to love and those who support us, we also need to be able to give love," says Dr. Janet Taylor, a psychiatrist, life coach, and clinical instructor of psychiatry at the Columbia University–affiliated Harlem Hospital in New York. "Love is not just physical or erotic love, it's the capacity to listen, to be curious about other people, to care enough about them that you ask questions and show an interest in their lives, and to understand how they think and what they value, which means you have to have some amount of engagement and awareness."

Of course, quality, not quantity, is important when it comes to close connections. Some people cast a wide social net but still can feel lonely. "It's not that the more socially connected you are the healthier you are," says Dr. Gail Saltz, a psychiatrist, author of *Becoming Real*, the mental health contributor on the *Today* show, and associate professor of psychiatry at NewYork-Presbyterian Hospital/Weill Cornell School of Medicine. "Some people are great if they have one friend, and that's fine. You need important relationships that you can be open in, but choose them carefully—you can't open yourself up to just anyone."

{health and marriage}

• In 2004 the Centers for Disease Control and Prevention released findings from a three-year study of 127,000 adults. It found that married people were healthier and happier than those who were divorced, widowed, single, or living with a partner. According to the report, married people were less likely to have back pain, headaches, and psychological stress, and they were less likely to smoke or drink excessively. The only downside: Married men, particularly those in middle age, were more prone to be overweight or obese.

• In 2006 psychologists at the University of Utah released a three-year study of 150 older married couples that found that when spouses showed hostile or controlling behavior to each other during disagreements, they were more likely to experience hardening of the arteries. Interestingly, wives were more at risk when their behavior or their husband's behavior was hostile; husbands were more at risk when their behavior or their wife's behavior was controlling or dominant. ⬘

Surviving the Slings and Arrows:
A Sense of Control

Difficulties strengthen the mind,

as labor does the body.

—SENECA

We all go through disappointments, struggles, losses, failures, and painful times over the course of our lives. But not all of us react to these experiences in the same way. Some people can go through horrible ordeals and seem to gain strength from them, while others can become immobilized by even minor setbacks. Why do some people cope better than others with adversity? Mental health experts say the reason is that they feel a sense of personal control. A sense of control is not about controlling others or outside circumstances. It is about inner power—the ability to manage our emotional response to difficult situations and the ability to know when we can change things and when we can't. The essentials for a sense of control are:

A strong belief in your own capabilities
Resilience
Optimism and humor
A sense of purpose

Why We Need a Sense of Control

Life is full of uncertainties; that's a fact. It could be the unexpected death of a loved one, the diagnosis of a serious illness, or a natural disaster. It could even be the annoyances of daily living—be it at work, at home, or on the road. While we can't always control external circumstances, we can control our responses to them.

"Based on a lot of recent research, both in neuroscience and cognitive and psychological science, one of the factors that really seems to be the key to developing and maintaining a healthy mind is a sense of control," says David H. Barlow, Ph.D., a professor of psychology and psychiatry and director of the Center for Anxiety and Related Disorders at Boston University. "It is the sense that you're going to be able to cope with and handle the various challenges, threats, and stresses that come at you in life. It may not always be easy, but you have a sense that you're going to be able to cope with them."

Those who believe in their ability to cope with strife (known as self-efficacy) are better equipped to adapt to change and withstand stress. "We've noticed through a lot of different studies that all healthy people have this, which means they are more resilient to trauma," says Dr. Barlow. "So if you have serious surgery, you will be released from the hospital sooner, you will recover more quickly, and your wounds will heal more quickly. Or if you lose your job, for instance, you tend to attribute it to other factors rather than your own inadequacy."

All humans have a deep need to feel a sense of control over their lives. Those who lack adequate coping skills are more vulnerable to the effects of stress. When we feel overwhelmed by life's burdens, it fosters feelings of helplessness, hopelessness, and victimization, which can lead to depression. Chronic stress is also linked to a laundry list of physical problems, including stomach ailments, high blood pressure, headaches, insomnia, and weight gain.

People who feel a sense of control see difficulties as challenges to confront, not as threats to be avoided. They adapt to change and take a proactive rather than a passive approach to problems.

"It could even be small things," says Dr. Gail Saltz, mental health contributor on the *Today* show, author of *Becoming Real: Defeating the Stories We Tell Ourselves That Hold Us Back* and *Anatomy of a Secret Life,* and associate professor of psychiatry at NewYork-Presbyterian Hospital/Weill Cornell School of Medicine. "It's your ability to say, 'Okay, that didn't work out well,' or 'This is difficult,' but I have this ability in me to manage it, to get through it, to learn from it and move on."

Essentials: What the Experts Say

Do you want a greater sense of control in your life? Here are the essential components:

A strong belief in your own capabilities. Known as self-efficacy, this is the belief system we hold about our own ability to bring about outcomes through our actions.

"Self-efficacy means that you have the sense that you are in control of things, that you have the skills to be effective in dealing with whatever comes at you in life," says Dr. Barlow.

Experts say it is how we perceive a difficult situation, no matter how big or small, that is critical to our emotional response. In other words, if we think that something is stressful, we will react with that emotion. Research shows that people with strong self-efficacy don't avoid problems or wait passively for solutions. They are adaptable and flexible when facing adverse situations and take a proactive approach through problem solving. As a result, they handle stress better because they feel they are in control. They also give themselves credit even for small accomplishments, and when they suffer setbacks, they don't belittle themselves with negative self-talk.

Believing in your own capabilities means giving yourself a pat on the back. "Even when good things happen, how do you process and understand that?" says Dr. Janet Taylor, a psychiatrist, life coach, and clinical instructor of psychiatry at the Columbia University–affiliated Harlem Hospital in New York. "Do you attribute it to your own power, or do you think it was just luck, or through someone else's power? I think the ability to realize that you have the power to create your own happiness is important."

Self-efficacy is particularly important as we age. Studies suggest that older people who feel a higher sense of personal control are happier and have fewer health and memory problems.

Resilience. In the 1936 movie *Swing Time*, Ginger Rogers tells Fred Astaire in the classic Jerome Kern song to "pick yourself up, dust yourself off, start all over again." That is sort of what resilience is—your ability to bounce back from adversity and to move forward. "Resilience means that you are able to absorb the impact of stresses, and even trauma, and come out of it without psychological damage," says Dr. Barlow.

When you have a sense of personal control, you have resilience. Resilience is about coping skills, survival. "It is very important," says Dr. Saltz. "If I had to bestow one trait, one gift, upon anyone, my number-one choice would be resilience because life always throws you curve balls. Inevitably something in your life will go wrong and become difficult and a struggle. Resilience is your ability to recoup, persevere, and bounce back. It is one of the best traits you could have in terms of your mental health."

People who are resilient are perseverant—they don't give up easily, and when they have failures or setbacks, they see them as learning experiences.

"Whatever you do in life, you're inevitably going to bump up against something that's difficult, something you didn't expect," says Dr. Michael Craig Miller, a psychiatrist, assistant professor of psychiatry at Harvard Medical School, and editor in chief of *The Harvard Mental Health Letter*. "Let's say you get the dream job and you're very happy for a while. But then you get into it and you realize you weren't even aware of what the challenges were. There may be an impulse to say, 'I made a mistake.' But you have to stay engaged, work things through."

An important component in resiliency is the ability to face and overcome fear, says Dr. Janet Taylor. "Many of us are creatures of habit who don't like to leave our comfort zones. But when you're fearful—by holding back or avoiding or canceling something—you're not being fully engaged in your life and you're missing an opportunity to develop your strengths. Even if you've had a bad experience and have to repeat the experience again, the best thing you can do is acknowledge that you're afraid but do it anyway, go back and reframe it and get a different perspective. By doing the things you fear, you gain confidence and power. When you have survived, you realize at some point that there's nothing to be afraid of."

Resilience has been the subject of much research, says Dr. Joan Borysenko, a psychologist and the author of *Your Soul's Compass: What Is Spiritual Guidance?* and *The Power of the Mind to Heal* and *Minding the Body, Mending the Mind*. Dr. Borysenko speaks of the work of the psychologist Suzanne Ouellette, Ph.D., who did research on coping skills and stress. "She studied hardiness in the face of stress, which has great overlap with resiliency—it may even be a synonym for it," says Dr. Borysenko. "She found that there were three essential characteristics of people who were hardy in the face of stress. She called them the three C's: control, commitment, and challenge. She said that hardy personalities (1) have a good sense of what control is—they don't make the mistake of trying to control what is inherently uncontrollable; instead they find something they can control and put energy there, (2) make a commitment to something that makes life meaningful, whether it's work or faith, and (3) see difficulty as a challenge rather than as a threat."

Optimism and humor. Having a strong sense of control goes hand and hand with optimism—the belief that things will work out for the best because of our efforts. "Optimism is the sense that basically you can cope with anything that comes along and everything is going to turn out all right, that everything's under control," says Dr. Barlow. "It's very protective. It's the positive expression of a sense of control." The attitude of optimism toward the outcome of events is often self-fulfilling. When we believe that things are going to work out for the best through our efforts and persistence, we stay motivated to bring about success.

Dr. Borysenko talks of the work of Martin E. P. Seligman, Ph.D., a pioneer in the development of positive psychology, a growing field of psychology that believes people can learn to be more optimistic and, therefore, happier.

"It's quite remarkable that you can actually teach yourself to think more optimistically," says Dr. Borysenko. "It starts with the capacity for awareness and self-reflection so that when something difficult happens you're actually able to notice your thought pattern. If you notice what it is and recognize that it's not leading in a good direction, that awareness opens up the possibility of making another choice in how you think. Of course, it's not easy."

It's not easy, especially if you're a pessimist. "I wouldn't say your mental health is bad if you're a pessimist," says Dr. Saltz. "But I would say that optimists are more hopeful, their physical health is better, and they tend to be less stressed, so it's preferable to be an optimist. Having said that, I think it's tough to make yourself an optimist if you're not. There's some wiring likely involved, so you have to work with what you've got, but yes, being an optimist is a nice asset."

Having a sense of humor goes hand in hand with optimism. By not taking life or ourselves too seriously and finding ways to laugh at our problems and foibles, we cope better with adversity and feel a greater sense of control. Mark Twain once said, "Humor is the great thing, the saving thing. The minute it crops up, all our irritation and resentments slip away, and a sunny spirit takes their place."

"It's good not to take life too seriously," says Dr. Taylor. "Let's face it, there are times when you just have to laugh at things and not take it personally."

A sense of purpose. Mental health experts say that when people feel personal control, it gives their lives a sense of purpose—a reason for being. We all need to feel that our lives have meaning and value. Everyone needs "to feel that some aspect of their lives has worth and that they are here for some purpose," says Dr. Janet Taylor. "What that purpose is comes from a different base for everyone. For some it might be from faith, that no matter how difficult things are, a higher power is going to help them find a way. For others it might be through service, giving of themselves to help other people. And for others, especially if they've had difficult lives, it might even be an attitude of 'in spite of'—'in spite of everything that has happened, I know that I can face the world, that my life has value and I'm going to show them.'" A sense of purpose is very important because "if you don't have it, life can feel very empty."

{the healing power of forgiveness}

Bad things can happen in life. When we've been hurt or victimized in some way, it can shatter our sense of trust in the world and result in feelings of anger, resentment, or vengeance. But when we can't let go of these powerful emotions, they can take a toxic toll on our health and well-being.

Through forgiveness we can learn to heal and move on, says Dr. Frederic Luskin, a pioneer in the study of forgiveness, author of *Forgive for Good* and *Forgive for Love*, and founder of the Stanford University Forgiveness Project and codirector of the Stanford–Northern Ireland HOPE Project, two renowned research programs that study the effects of forgiveness intervention.

Forgiveness is the process of making peace with our past. It gives us "a different language about what happened, so the story about the experience changes," says Dr. Luskin.

Its opposite, unforgiveness, "comes from trying to control things you can't, like other people or the past," he comments. "And that's what sets in motion all this suffering. So when we think that other people shouldn't have behaved in a certain way, that's the initiator of unforgiveness."

But when we get stuck in this thinking year after year, we are the ones who suffer most. By focusing on our hurt, we give people power over us. One central reason "we teach people to forgive is that here they are wasting their lives, stewing over something that's over, that's done," Dr. Luskin says. "And the people who harmed them are fine or may not care or may not believe they were wrong, or might even be dead. So the only person forgiveness is for is you."

Forgiving does not mean forgetting or condoning bad behavior, however. "If somebody murders your son or daughter, there is no forgetting," according to Dr. Luskin. "But there are different levels of remembering, and different takes on the story, which forgiveness provides." You don't have to reconcile, either, in order to forgive. "You can forgive and not reconcile and you cannot forgive and reconcile. If you look at unhappily married couples, they reconcile but don't forgive all the time."

Forgiveness can't be rushed, of course. You have to

be ready to forgive, and that takes time. "The time is for the grief process, not for the forgiveness," says Dr. Luskin. "You're going to hurt, you're going to be sad, you're going to be angry—whatever the stages of grief are. When someone is taken from you or when some harm befalls you, there's no avoiding the pain of that."

The problem is when we get stuck in our pain and can't go forward. Unfortunately, some people condense their pain into a life story, Dr. Luskin observes. "They keep it going or work at finding an enemy to blame, and that's very different from normal grief. It's not always a conscious thing. Some people struggle to take responsibility for their current experience and would rather have an excuse for why they're failing at their life. But even if you have grief and struggle, you at some point have to say, 'This is my life, including this crappy thing that happened to me, and now how do I make the best of it?' Many people avoid that."

Holding on to resentments and anger for years on end reinforces feelings of victimization. "Long-term anger shows that you haven't done anything to figure out how to deal successfully with the situation," says Dr. Luskin. "It's a flare of 'I don't get it, I can't help myself, I'm helpless.' It's a false empowerment."

What is the impact on our health? "Mostly you can identify it as the negative effects of stress," he says. "If you're feeling anger, resentment, disappointment, or self-pity on a regular basis, it puts stress into your body every single time you feel those things. It has a cumulative effect and leads to stress-related disease. Anger is probably the harshest emotion that we can generate in our body—it is particularly toxic and inter-personally destructive. Not only do you stress yourself out, but you antagonize people around you. You cut yourself off to love and connection."

For more information on Dr. Luskin and his research on forgiveness, go to learningtoforgive.com.

{trauma: coping skills}

Experiencing a traumatic event—whether it's a natural disaster, a violent crime, or an accident of some kind—can have a serious impact on our mental and physical health, depending on how we deal with it. Initially we may have any number of symptoms, including flashbacks, anxiety, and sleeplessness. Here are some ways to cope:

• Understand that your symptoms may be normal, especially right after the trauma.

• Keep to your usual routine.

• Take the time to resolve day-to-day conflicts so they do not add to your stress.

• Do not shy away from situations, people, and places that remind you of the trauma.

• Find ways to relax and be kind to yourself.

• Turn to family, friends, and clergy for support, and talk about your experiences and feelings with them.

- Participate in leisure and recreational activities.

- Recognize that you cannot control everything.

- Recognize the need for trained help, and call a local mental health center. ⌯

Source: Adapted from materials from the Centers for Disease Control and Prevention

Living Consciously:
Mindfulness and Acceptance

The ability to be in the present moment is a major
component of mental wellness.

—ABRAHAM MASLOW

Many of us live our lives anywhere but here. Our thoughts
run on automatic pilot—preoccupied with one thing or another. We never seem to be in the present. We are essentially
mindless, controlled by force of habit. In contrast, when we
are mindful, we are fully engaged in the moment. We are
here, not there.

Mindfulness brings clarity. It leads to self-acceptance: We
begin to see ourselves as we are, but without judgment or
criticism. The concepts of mindfulness and acceptance are
rooted in Buddhist meditative practices that go back more
than 2,500 years. But you don't have to be a Buddhist to prac-

tice them—you can apply them to every area of your life. The essentials for mindfulness and acceptance are:

The ability to be present
The ability to observe without judgment or criticism
The capacity to notice new things

Why We Need Mindfulness and Acceptance

Over the last thirty years or so, with the growth of interest in mind-body medicine in the West, mindfulness—in the form of meditation, visualization, yoga, and other techniques—has gained wide acceptance as a way to reduce stress and enhance overall wellness. Early mindfulness practitioners include Jon Kabat-Zinn, Ph.D., who developed Mindfulness-Based Stress Reduction, and Dr. Herbert Benson, who developed the Relaxation Response.

The concept of mindfulness also has been integrated into various psychotherapies as a treatment for anxiety, depression, and mood disorders. One intervention attracting much interest is Acceptance and Commitment Therapy, developed by Steven C. Hayes, Ph.D., which uses mindfulness and acceptance techniques to help people identify troublesome thoughts that elicit pain and to evaluate them without judgment.

Mindfulness is being present and aware. When we are

mindful (here), we are fully engaged in the moment. When we are mindless (on automatic, not here), we think through force of habit, attaching meaning to thoughts or feelings that often have nothing to do with reality.

"You create your reality through what you think," says Joan Borysenko, Ph.D., a psychologist and author of *Your Soul's Compass: What Is Spiritual Guidance?* and *The Power of the Mind to Heal*. "I'm not using that in a New Age way at all. At any moment we can be in heaven or hell with the same circumstances, depending on where our mind is."

Unfortunately, our minds have a habit of going to the same old places. "Your mind is in a groove," she says. "The old wisdom traditions, Buddhism for example, have a word for it, called *samskara*, which is habit of mind, a thought pattern. It's like runoff on the top of a mountain. It's not going to run down wherever it chooses. It runs down in the groove that's been cut over time."

Basically, our minds are chatterboxes that produce an endless number of judgments and evaluations—called self-talk or internal dialogue—which we usually are unaware of but which directly influence our behavior. Much of this dialogue can be self-sabotaging.

"The contents of the mind, specifically the stories we tell ourselves, are arbitrary," says Martha Beck, a sociologist, columnist for *O: The Oprah Magazine*, and author of *Finding Your Own North Star: Claiming the Life You Were Meant to Live.* "Your verbal mind might as well be a roomful of chimpanzees hammering on word processors. Your brain produces thoughts in a stream of narrative just like—and I'm going to use an awful simile here, but it's apt—just like your intestines produce excrement. I like to use that instead of, say, your heart pumping blood, precisely because it's such a lowly example. You've got a lot of crap in your head and most of it isn't true."

We become aware of our thoughts through mindfulness, which leads to acceptance. "Acceptance is being able to put up with the distressing and unpleasant thoughts that often pop into our heads," says David H. Barlow, Ph.D., professor of psychology and psychiatry and director of the Center for Anxiety and Related Disorders at Boston University. "One of the characteristics of people with anxiety and depression is that they have a continual stream of unpleasant thoughts running through their heads. They can't stop worrying about something that's going to happen or maybe they're ruminating about something they did wrong and can't get it out of their heads."

But trying to control, eliminate, or avoid these thoughts has the opposite effect, he says. "What we've discovered is that with internal negative states like thoughts and feelings, the more you try to suppress them or try to distract yourself from them, the stronger they become," says Dr. Barlow. "Whereas if you take the opposite tack and develop a more accepting attitude—you are aware that those thoughts and feelings are there but you're able to push them off to the side of your mind, we tell patients to let them flow in one ear and out the other—then we find these thoughts and feelings begin to fade away and become less salient and much less intense."

When you practice acceptance, you observe your thoughts "in a nonjudgmental, nonemotional way," he says. "It's just being aware of 'Oh yeah, there's that thought again. But it's all right. I'm going on with this activity. I'm aware that it's there, but I'm going to passively ignore it as I go on with my life.' In other words, you're putting the feelings and thoughts to one side and you're saying, 'Yes, I know you're there, but right now I'm on to other things.'"

Through acceptance, says Beck, we begin to realize that the chatter in our mind is just that. "Once you have that epiphany—that your thoughts are just thoughts and that very often they don't correspond to anything—once you have that, you can never unring the bell."

Essentials: What the Experts Say

Mindfulness and acceptance are about awareness, being in the here and now, and seeing in a new way. To become more mindful and accepting, the essentials are:

The ability to be present. When we live in the future or past, we are living in our minds. This moment, right now, is the only one we have. Being present is taking notice—but not judging—and experiencing whatever happens in a new way.

How do we do that? Mindfulness meditation is one way—usually focusing on a single thing—the breath, for example—to keep yourself anchored in the present. "I think the ancient wisdom traditions have a lot to offer," Joan Borysenko says. "If you're able to turn off that inner dialogue for a while—whether you do it through meditation, qi gong, or yoga—it can raise your consciousness to create a gap for a moment between a behavior that's automatic and the potential to let go and move in another direction."

You can become more mindful in many other ways, says Ellen J. Langer, Ph.D., professor of psychology at Harvard University and a pioneer in the field of mindfulness research who has written several books on the subject, including *Mind-*

fulness, The Power of Mindful Learning and *On Becoming an Art-ist: Reinventing Yourself Through Mindful Creativity*, as well as more than two hundred research articles. Learn to practice mindfulness in everyday activities: eating, walking, washing dishes, bathing, reading, learning a new skill—whatever it is you're doing. "I know lots of people who can't sit still for ten minutes once a day, no less twenty minutes twice a day to meditate, so this is in some ways a much more Western approach to getting to the same place," she says. The point is to be fully engaged with whatever you are doing.

"When you're not dwelling in the future or past, you only have to deal with the present, and it's a lot easier to relax," says Martha Beck.

By being present, we are more open to learning new things. "When you're unfocused, you don't let other people in and you miss things," says Dr. Janet Taylor, a psychiatrist, life coach, and clinical instructor of psychiatry at the Co-lumbia University–affiliated Harlem Hospital in New York. "But when you're mindful, you're open and curious—and listening. You pick up all this wisdom by engaging in other people's lives. Some of the best learning I've had is from cabdrivers, people on the street, or random conversations when people tell you how they got where they are. Today we're so stressed that we don't let other people in and we only feel that we can learn from certain people. The reality is once you open yourself up, you can learn from anybody."

The ability to observe without judgment or criticism. When we are mindful, we take notice of our thoughts, but realize that there are no certainties, that things are always changing. We see that thoughts are just thoughts. "Most of your suffering comes from your narratives that aren't grounded in reality—they're just narratives," says Beck. "The condition of psychological freedom exists when you realize you are not the stream of stories in your mind."

Beck speaks of the Japanese Zen priest Shunryu Suzuki. "He said that the entire dogma of Zen can be summed up in three words: 'Not Always So.' " This means that no matter what you think, you may be wrong. "Once you have this in your mind, 'Not Always So,' you never really believe that anything is absolute," she says. "Not always so is a ticket out of negative stories and most of your suffering."

We gain perspective about ourselves by noticing thoughts but not taking them seriously. "When you observe your thoughts, you're watching, which is different from thinking," says Beck. "You regard your thoughts with a kind of amusement from a place that is not thought-based." This, she says, can be difficult for some Westerners to do. "When Descartes said, 'I think, therefore I am,' he was stating a rationalist belief that we *are* our thoughts. But we're not."

Most cultures, she says, have traditions for stepping outside of thoughts. "In the Sioux Indian tradition one of the metaphors for the mind is a wolf that chases its own tail and goes round and round like crazy. It's a very intelligent animal, but it becomes crazy when it just focuses on itself. Some Asian cultures call it 'monkey mind,' this apelike thing that chitters and chatters. In almost every wisdom culture, there is the tradition of laughing at the mind. But rationalism says, 'No, no, no—the mind is our identity.' So we are always mired in thought."

How can you free yourself from "monkey mind"? "Don't take your thoughts seriously," she says. Above all, don't be judgmental. "Be kind and compassionate to the one who is thinking ridiculous thoughts."

The capacity to notice new things. When we are mindless, we see things in a limited way, through habit or routine. "Things are constantly changing, yet we hold them still in our minds," Dr. Langer says. When we are mindful and tuned in, we begin to realize that we really don't know what we think we know. We begin to see that things are "Not Always So."

"I define mindfulness as the process of actively noticing new things—it doesn't matter if what you notice is smart or silly, as long as it's new for you," she says. "If you don't remember to actively notice new things, the other step is to recognize that there are no certainties."

Being mindful means not letting our present be controlled by our past. "You have to recognize that evaluations are in our heads, not in the things we are evaluating," Dr. Langer says. "The more mindful one is, the more aware one becomes of the various evaluations anything can take." When we are mindful, we begin to see that there are many ways of looking at things, that there are alternatives to old ways of thinking.

{mindlessness versus mindfulness}

To understand mindfulness, think of its opposite: mindlessness. That concept was what initially caught the attention of Ellen J. Langer, Ph.D., a professor of psychology at Harvard University and a renowned pioneer in the field of mindfulness. Back in the mid-1970s, when Dr. Langer arrived at the university from New York City, she began to observe some unusual behavior.

"Cambridge is full of smart people, but I noticed that they did the strangest things," she said. "For instance, you'd walk into a bank and there would be four tellers, and three of the lines would be full and one line would have nobody in it. In New York, everyone would've rushed to be in that other line. So I thought, 'There's something strange happening, people just don't seem to be here.' So that's when I first started looking at mindlessness. And from there, it was a very short jump to mindfulness."

Since then, Dr. Langer has written many books on the subject, including *Mindfulness, The Power of Mind-*

ful Learning, and *On Becoming an Artist: Reinventing Yourself Through Mindful Creativity*, as well as more than two hundred research articles. She says mindfulness is "the process of actively noticing new things. When you're actively noticing new things, it puts you in the present. It's the feeling of engagement."

On the other hand, mindlessness is when "you're relying on distinctions that have already been drawn," she says. "Your present is controlled by your past. You're insensitive to context and perspective and your rules and routines govern rather than just guide. So even if they no longer serve the original purpose, you're oblivious to that and you just keep doing the same things over and over. Mindlessness usually comes about by default, not by design."

When you're not "here," people—and animals— know it, she says. To demonstrate the power of mindful versus mindless behavior, Dr. Langer describes a research experiment she did with dolphins and their trainers. "We instructed the trainers to be mindful or mindless. Those trained to be mindful were told to think about how that dolphin is different from all the other dolphins and how

he's different today from the last time they inter-
acted with him. Those trained to be mindless were
told to think about all the things they know to be
true about dolphins, all the certainties, which is
equivalent to mindless understanding." The result?
"When the trainers were instructed to be mindful,
the dolphins swam to them faster and stayed with
them longer than when the trainers were mindless,"
she says.

{eating consciously}

When it comes to food, is your brain on automatic? Researchers say people often overeat—even
when food isn't tasty or satisfying—because of emotional, not physical, hunger. Mindfulness can be
an effective tool in helping people become aware
of their relationship with food, says leading re-
searcher Jean L. Kristeller, Ph.D., director of the
Center for the Study of Health, Religion and Spiri-

tuality at Indiana State University and founder of the Mindfulness-Based Eating Awareness Training program. For more than twenty years, Dr. Kristeller has studied how mindfulness techniques help people with obesity and eating disorders.

She says there are three critical elements to mindful eating:

1. *Awareness of hunger cues.* "You need to be able to distinguish between physical hunger and emotional hunger," she says. "We work with a ten-point scale. We ask people before every meal to take a few moments of mindfulness to notice how hungry they are, with ten being as hungry as you could possibly be and one being not hungry at all. What we've found is that it's remarkable how quickly people can distinguish between different levels of hunger this way. Also, become attuned to your emotional pulls for food—do you tend to eat more when you're angry, bored, anxious, or depressed?"

2. *Awareness of fullness cues.* "Know what your satiety is—what is the point of fullness that works for you?" she says. "Again, we use the ten-point scale. We have

found that for many heavy individuals this is mind opening. Within a matter of a few weeks, they say, 'I ate lunch yesterday to a four, and I ate dinner to a six, and I felt so much better.' "

3. *Awareness of satisfaction.* "Become more attuned to your satisfaction around every bite of food so that you're satisfied with the quality rather than the quantity," she says. "We use the word 'savor'—savor the experience of food, the taste, the smell. Even if it's in small amounts, eat mindfully and with full appreciation."

Dr. Kristeller says it's not about deprivation but balance. "Don't say, 'I'm never going to have chocolate ice cream' if you really love it, because that isn't going to work for you. Think more in terms of 'How can I keep on having chocolate ice cream but keep it in balance of how I use food that works for me?' So, eating a few tablespoons of Ben & Jerry's New York Super Fudge Chunk with complete mindfulness of pleasure may be more satisfying than eating a cup of fat-free sherbet— and you can still end up with the same number of calories." 🖰

Lifting the Fog: The Ability to Be Real

It takes courage to grow up and become who you really are.

—E. E. CUMMINGS

Who are you, really? Many of us don't have a clue. No matter what we do, we never feel that we get it right, whether it's our careers or our relationships. We may feel numb, like we are going through the motions of life, doing what we're supposed to do instead of what we want to do. We may not even know what we want to do. Authenticity is about knowing ourselves—and that includes our strengths as well as our weaknesses. It is about using our talents and abilities to full expression. It is about finding our truth. It isn't an easy journey, but it is worth it. The payoff: a life of meaning and passion instead of a life of mediocrity and compromise. The essentials for being real are:

Honest self-reflection

The capacity to express and feel unpleasant emotions

Acceptance of self and others, warts and all

The courage to live your own life

Why We Need to Be Real

We all wear masks of a sort; it is how we learn to function and protect ourselves in the world. But often we lose touch with what's behind the mask. Being authentic is "knowing the difference between your true self and your false self," says Dr. Michael Craig Miller, a psychiatrist and the editor in chief of the *Harvard Mental Health Letter*. "Whatever it is you're showing to the world, however you present yourself, it's having a consciousness about who you really are and what matters. It's not that we're all acting, but there are some people who never really have a sense of where their own inner life begins and ends."

What is true self and false self? They are subjects that have been written about for decades. Basically, we are all born with a true self, the vital essence of who we really are. At the same time, we are also born with the need to be loved and recognized by our parents. But not everyone gets those needs met. When that happens, we adapt and conform by hiding our needs, and we develop a false self in order to survive in our world. We are not aware of the false self—it's part of our unconscious mind.

"It's not that we don't want to be authentic," says Joan Borysenko, Ph.D., a psychologist and author of *The Power of the Mind to Heal* and *Your Soul's Compass: What Is Spiritual Guidance?* "It's just that we are trying our very hardest to be loved and to be happy. It's from the fundamental need to be loved."

We can lose touch with our true selves by the pressure to conform and fit in. "There are so many ways we lose our authenticity," Dr. Borysenko says. "Look at all the people who lose authenticity because of religious teachings, when so much of who they are that doesn't fit into the mold gets stored away. Or because of societal things, like it's not nice for a woman to be angry. It also comes from gender things and from the culture—whether it's the culture of the workplace or the culture of your family. Both men and women are prone to live their lives in a state of near unconsciousness where a great deal of what we think is not going to get us the love that we need, so it gets stored away."

The result is that our true self can become obscured. We don't feel comfortable in our own skin; we are living a life that is not our own. "People try to be someone they're not, and they feel like fakes," says Dr. Gail Saltz, a psychiatrist, author of *Becoming Real*, and the mental health contributor on the *Today* show. On the other hand, she says, "Authenticity is your ability to be real, to know who you really are and to accept who you really are."

In her book Dr. Saltz says that as little children we make up narratives or stories to compensate for the pain and lack of control we felt in our young world. "Our stories tell us who we are and how the world operates," she writes. "We create these stories out of necessity. They explain events in our lives that are traumatic and difficult, and they allowed us to hold on to those we loved when they either did not or could not respond to our most essential need to be loved and recognized."

But these narratives are false, based on the interpretations of a child. The trouble, Dr. Saltz says, is that as adults we still believe them. In her book she lists many types of self-defeating stories we tell ourselves, including, "I need to be 'good' so everyone will like me," "I have to be perfect, or something bad will happen," "There must be something wrong with me because no one stays around," and "If I'm not number one, then I'm nothing at all." But, she says, these narratives are not who we are at all, and they cause us great pain, limiting us and preventing us from being authentic.

These narratives get set in our unconscious mind. It

is through awareness that we identify the negative inner dialogue—the stories we tell ourselves—and begin to think in a new way. Why do we need to be authentic? Because it means finding truth and freedom, being the person we were meant to be.

Essentials: What the Experts Say

To become a more authentic, real person, the essentials are:

Honest self-reflection. The road to authenticity is a journey of the mind and soul. Who am I? Where am I going? What do I want out of life? What are my real values? You are the only person who can answer these questions, but it requires time and looking inward, which means getting still and quiet with ourselves—not an easy thing to do for many people.

In today's world we spend a good deal of our lives in a whirlwind of busyness—with too much noise, too many distractions, too many things to do. While having a full life is a wonderful thing, filling every moment with activity can be a way to avoid looking at ourselves. "As soon as you stop running, what happens to so many people is that the emptiness, the anxiety, the doubt, the fear, the depression are there like a fog," says Dr. Borysenko. "Keeping busy clearly keeps you out of touch with some of that fog. Busyness can be a form of self-medication in the same way that drinking or drugging is."

How can you deepen your connection with yourself? First, keep a daily journal of your feelings, thoughts, and dreams. Also, try to cultivate stillness by practicing meditation, yoga, or some type of contemplative practice—it is in the silence that you hear your true voice. Listen to your inner dialogue—you know, the narrative that plays over and over in your head. What kinds of things do you say to yourself? Are they harsh, hurtful, judgmental, and overly critical statements? Once you become aware of those negative narratives, you can begin to change them. Awareness is the operative word here.

The capacity to express and feel uncomfortable emotions.
There's no getting away from it: Life has painful moments. We have to allow ourselves to feel negative emotions like anger or sadness—it's part of being human. When we don't acknowledge and feel these emotions, by hiding them or denying them, it can prevent us from knowing ourselves and being happy. "We have to have tolerance for uncomfortable emotions," says Dr. Saltz. People who avoid feeling unpleasant emotions "either get flooded or overwhelmed or they

have to stuff them away until they explode in some symptom," she says. "People will do anything not to feel unhappy, and that generally leads to problems." When we get in touch with our feelings, particularly something painful from the past—whether it's anger, resentment, or sadness—it can be the key that unlocks the door to self-knowledge and, ultimately, happiness. She says that when we have the courage to face these emotions we give ourselves the chance to connect with the powerful unconscious mind—the place where negative stories about ourselves originate. (Note: If you have any serious or unresolved issues with your past, it's advisable to seek psychological counseling.)

Acceptance of self and others, warts and all. One surefire way to sabotage authenticity is perfectionism. Putting unreasonable demands on ourselves and others is a setup for disappointment and unhappiness. Simply, it's a no-win deal: We will never measure up; we will never be good enough. Being real is about being human. When we are authentic, we acknowledge our strengths and our courage as well as our vulnerabilities and weaknesses. We accept that we are not perfect and that we don't have to know everything; and when we do make mistakes, we have the courage to admit we are wrong. By letting go of perfectionism, we become

less judgmental of ourselves. Above all, we learn to be forgiving. "You cannot beat yourself up—you have to forgive
yourself," says Dr. Borysenko. "If you walk around in a cloud
of regret, regretting what you've done, regretting who you
are, regretting your choices, there's no question that you will
be a very unhappy person."

"We need to examine ourselves and our life experiences in a
way that doesn't cause too much guilt or self-blame," says Dr.
Taylor. "We have so many stages and transitions in life—it's
all part of a process. What you accept and understand about
yourself at age twenty is a lot different from when you're forty.
Building on your experiences, both positive and negative, leads
to self-knowledge that, hopefully, we all get before we die. I
think the major challenge of life is to say, 'I get myself and
I get the world, and I accept it all.' " A big plus: When we
become more accepting and forgiving of ourselves, we also
become more accepting and forgiving toward others.

The courage to live your own life. The critical payoff to being authentic is that you are living your life creatively and
with passion. You are being the person you were meant to
be and doing what you were meant to do. "Authenticity is
a great way to describe what's being expressed in your
relationships, in your work, and in your creativity," says

Dr. Miller of the *Harvard Mental Health Letter*. "I think that when you are able to express yourself through whatever mode you've chosen or wherever your talents have led you to, it is one of the most meaningful and satisfying things in your life. Whether you write a book or play the piano, it doesn't matter what it is. I'm not talking about fine art. You can live a creative life as an accountant, or as an athlete, a doctor, or a lawyer."

{getting to know you 101}

The topic of authenticity has been a central theme throughout history. Here are some famous and infamous quotes on the subject:

This above all, to thine own self be true.
—WILLIAM SHAKESPEARE, FROM *Hamlet*

There is just one life for each of us: our own.
—EURIPIDES

Be who you are and say what you feel because those who mind don't matter and those who matter don't mind.—DR. SEUSS

The only tyrant I accept in this world is the still voice within.—MAHATMA GANDHI

Most powerful is he who has himself in his own power.—SENECA

Your vision will become clear only when you look into your heart.—CARL JUNG

Resolve to be thyself; and know, that he who finds himself, loses his misery.—MATTHEW ARNOLD

Look well into thyself; there is a source of strength which will always spring up if thou wilt always look there.—MARCUS AURELIUS

Always be a first-rate version of yourself, instead of a second-rate version of somebody else.
—JUDY GARLAND

Observe all men, thyself most.
—BENJAMIN FRANKLIN

No one can give you better advice than yourself.
—CICERO

Seek out that particular mental attribute which makes you feel most deeply and vitally alive, along

with which comes the inner voice which says,
"This is the real me," and when you have found
that attitude, follow it.—WILLIAM JAMES

Don't compromise yourself. You're all you've got.
—BETTY FORD

Knowing others is intelligence; knowing yourself is true wisdom. Mastering others is strength;
mastering yourself is true power.
—TAO TE CHING

No bird soars too high, if he soars on his own
wings.—WILLIAM BLAKE

The thing that is really hard, and really amazing, is
giving up on being perfect and beginning to work
on becoming yourself.—ANNA QUINDLEN

To be nobody but yourself in a world which
is doing its best, night and day, to make you
everybody else means to fight the hardest battle
which any human being can fight; and never stop
fighting.—E. E. CUMMINGS

Most people are other people. Their thoughts are
someone else's opinions, their lives a mimicry,

their passions a quotation.—OSCAR WILDE, FROM
De Profundis

Let the world know you as you are, not as you
think you should be, because sooner or later, if
you are posing, you will forget the pose, and then
where are you?—FANNY BRICE ⚲

Mind Fitness: Physical and Mental Exercise

An active mind cannot exist in an inactive body.

—GENERAL GEORGE PATTON

We all know that our bodies need physical exercise to function well, but so do our minds. A healthy mind requires a healthy brain, which is the organ of the mind. Over the last few decades there have been many studies on the benefits of physical exercise on the brain, and in recent years a growing body of research is showing that mental exercise—using spiritual techniques like meditation or participating in challenging activities—also has beneficial effects on the brain. The essentials for physical and mental exercise are:

Regular physical activity
Meditation and other mental exercise

Why Our Brains Need Exercise

Your brain is a complex organ that needs regular activity and stimulation to stay healthy. Most of us are familiar with the benefits of physical exercise on our bodies; among other things, it reduces the risk of high blood pressure, osteoporosis, obesity, diabetes, cardiovascular disease, stroke, and certain cancers. Regular exercise also offers significant benefits to the brain.

The latest research has found that exercise has long-lasting effects on the brain, says Dr. Michael Craig Miller, editor in chief of the *Harvard Mental Health Letter* and an assistant professor of psychiatry at Harvard Medical School. Regular exercise, he says, improves your mood, decreases anxiety, improves sleep, improves resilience in the face of stress, and raises self-esteem. Some research, he says, suggests exercise also may improve cognitive skills like memory and may even decrease the risk of age-related mental illnesses like dementia and Alzheimer's disease. "The brain needs exercise the way the rest of the body needs it," says Dr. Miller. "Exercise helps your brain stay healthy. And a healthy brain is required if you're going to have a healthy mind."

Studies also show that exercise helps combat depression. "One of the things we need for a healthy mind is exercise," says Joan Borysenko, Ph.D., a psychologist and the author of *Your Soul's Compass: What Is Spiritual Guidance?* and *The Power of the Mind to Heal.* "It's really clear from the research on depression that the best antidepressant is exercise." A well-known study at Duke University in 2000 suggests that regular exercise can be as effective as antidepressants in treating depression.

Anxiety and depression are a significant problem in this country: About 40 million Americans have some kind of anxiety disorder and 18.8 million suffer from depression, with women having twice the risk as men, according to the National Institute of Mental Health.

Aside from regular physical exercise, a healthy mind also needs mental stimulation in order to stay fit. Contrary to what most people think, the brain is not static—in fact, it has natural plasticity, meaning it has the capacity to remodel itself in response to new experiences at any time throughout our lives. Some neuroscientists say that by doing certain mind-based activities, you can bring about positive changes in the brain. For instance, recent studies have shown that techniques like meditation actually change our brains.

One of the pioneers in this research is Richard J. Davidson, Ph.D., a neuroscientist and the director of the W. M.

Keck Laboratory for Functional Brain Imaging and Behavior at the University of Wisconsin in Madison. Through the encouragement of the Dalai Lama, in the early 1990s Dr. Davidson began to investigate the effects of meditation on brain function by measuring electrical activity in the brains of Tibetan monks while they meditated. He found that the monks had especially high activity in the left prefrontal cortex, an area of the brain linked with positive emotions like happiness. Over many years of study, Dr. Davidson says that through the practice of spiritual disciplines like meditation we can rewire the brain's circuitry and increase happiness as well as improve attention, memory, and focus.

"I think that regular exercise of the mind is absolutely crucial because in my view, and this is the view that we believe is supported by modern research, qualities like happiness and well-being should best be regarded as skills that can be trained," says Dr. Davidson. "The idea that we all have a kind of fixed level of happiness or grumpiness is totally inconsistent with modern scientific evidence. In this culture we pay very little attention to the cultivation of these qualities as skills, and I think there is a lot to be learned by regarding them as skills. I think it offers a very hopeful message for people, and it's clearly based on solid evidence that indicates that we can change our brains by transforming our minds."

Essentials: What the Experts Say

To get your mind in tip-top shape, the essentials are:

Regular physical activity. The evidence is clear: Physical exercise is good for your mind. Among other benefits, it increases the flow of oxygen-rich blood to the brain, which makes you more alert and improves your ability to concentrate; it raises the levels of serotonin, a mood-elevating neurotransmitter in the brain; it also raises levels of dopamine, a neurotransmitter associated with the pleasure system in the brain; and it stimulates the production of new brain cells (neurons) in the hippocampus, an area of the brain associated with memory.

How much exercise do you need, and what type is best? According to Dr. Michael Craig Miller of the *Harvard Mental Health Letter*, at least thirty minutes a day about five times a week of any type of moderate exercise—either aerobic or strength training—has beneficial effects on the brain. "It doesn't matter what you do, as long as you do something," says Dr. Miller. "Research shows that doing something is better than doing nothing. The key is to keep doing it. Be consistent. Exercising a manageable amount every day—or several days a week—is much better than being overambitious and then giving up."

If you're a couch potato and hate the thought of exercise, the easiest way to start moving is to take a walk. It's easy, doesn't require training or equipment, and can be done pretty much anywhere. More and more research shows that walking benefits body and mind. Among other things, it may decrease the risk for developing heart disease, breast cancer, and diabetes, maintains weight, controls blood pressure, lowers bad cholesterol, and builds bone and muscle. It also reduces stress, elevates mood, eases symptoms of depression, and improves sleep. Another plus: Walking is meditative—it helps clear the mind. Got a problem? Do what the ancient Romans did. *Solvitur ambulando* is a Latin proverb meaning "It is solved by walking."

Meditation and other mental exercise. Like the muscles in our bodies, the muscles in our minds need regular workouts, too. Spiritual techniques like daily meditation—using visualization and deep breathing—can improve our minds.

"The brain becomes more awake, attentive, and alert," says Dr. Davidson. "The change that is produced in the brain is associated with increased efficiency and increased activation in certain regions of the brain that we know to be involved in attention and the regulation of emotion."

But there are many types of meditation, and they are not all the same. "The word 'meditation' is kind of like the word 'sports.' It refers to a whole variety of practices that don't necessarily produce comparable sorts of changes," he says. "We have studied a variety of different kinds of practices from the Buddhist tradition. We have been particularly interested in meditation that is designed to cultivate compassion and in meditation designed to improve one's attention to facilitate concentration and focus."

Do other contemplative techniques like prayer have the same effect? "We don't know scientifically," says Dr. Davidson. "There may be certain kinds of meditation and certain kinds of prayer that share some similarities, although we don't know that with any certainty from the scientific research to date, primarily because there has been virtually no good research on the brain changes associated with prayer."

How often should you meditate? "The data suggest that every little bit helps," he says. "Many people once said they didn't have time for physical exercise, but now they have figured out a way to build it in to their weekly routine. I would argue that even a very short amount of meditation practice, even ten minutes, can produce beneficial effects. And if a person was so busy that they insisted they had no time, I would say sleep ten minutes less. Meditation will be much more beneficial than that additional ten minutes of sleep."

Aside from practices like meditation, your mind needs stimulation through activities that involve challenge such as problem solving and learning new things—for instance, traveling to a new environment, learning to play an instrument, learning to speak a new language, or taking up a creative pursuit like painting. (For more information on ways to improve mind fitness, see "Use It or Lose It: Active Mind, Healthy Mind," page 314.)

{can you learn to be happy?}

Yes, says Tal Ben-Shahar, Ph.D., the author of *Happier: Learn the Secrets to Daily Joy and Lasting Fulfillment* and a lecturer at Harvard whose class in positive psychology is the most popular course at the university. He says there are guiding principles to happiness, based on solid research. But the quest can be elusive for some people because they keep looking in the wrong places.

"It never ceases to amaze me that, despite evidence to the contrary—and when I say evidence I mean scientific evidence and personal evidence—people still live under the assumption that money or power will make them happy," says Dr. Ben-Shahar. Some people believe happiness is found in external circumstances, "waiting for that one thing. It could be the knight in shining armor, the guru with the secret, or the book with the answer—what I call the fairy-tale approach to happiness—or it could be the next promotion or raise. People will think, 'Okay, the last three promotions didn't make me happy, but the next one will.'"

But true and lasting happiness comes from within, he says. How do you get the real thing? Dr. Ben-Shahar offers these principles:

Cultivate experiences that offer pleasure and meaning. Dr. Ben-Shahar defines happiness as "the overall experience of pleasure and meaning." He says that when experiences—through our relationships or our work—"provide us with a sense of purpose as well as a sense of joy, we experience happiness."

Exercise regularly. "Studies show that regular exercise—and that could be as little as three times a week—has the same impact as antidepressant drugs," he says. "Exercise changes our mood—not just when the endorphins are kicking in but because it affects our overall sense of well-being."

Express gratitude. "The word 'appreciate' has two meanings," Dr. Ben-Shahar points out. "The first is to say thank you, not to take something for granted. The second meaning is to grow—for example, when money appreciates in the bank. In other words, when we appreciate things—whether it's our relationships, ourselves, or the world—the good grows."

Practice meditation. When we practice meditation regularly, "we change the way our brain functions, making us more susceptible to positive emotions and more resilient in the face of painful emotions. Meditate for as little as fifteen minutes a day, or do yoga three times a week." Meditation helps us stay in the present moment, and that contributes to our psychological as well as our physical well-being.

Develop positive habits or rituals. Change can be very difficult for people, and most efforts fail. "Self-discipline is not enough," Dr. Ben-Shahar says. "In order to make change last beyond the temporary, it's important to get rituals in place to keep the momentum going. You have to create a habit. Do things that are meaningful and important to you, and do them consistently. Once the habit is formed, it's no longer difficult to maintain. The consensus is that it takes about thirty days to form a new habit, but once it's in place, we have less difficulty maintaining it."

Accept that life has ups and downs. Painful emotions are part of life, Dr. Ben-Shahar says. "One of the main ideas in my course is to give ourselves the permission to be human. There is a misconception that a happy life is a life of constant highs, which is a misunderstanding of what happiness is. In fact, a happy and fulfilling life is one with constant ups and downs—it's natural. Painful emotions are as much a part of nature as the law of gravity. When we don't accept and feel these emotions, they only become more dominant."

Take time to smell the roses. Try to simplify your life by slowing down. "When you try to do more and more things in less and less time, you wind up not enjoying anything," Dr. Ben-Shahar says. "Take your time. Become like a wine connoisseur— look at the color of the wine, smell it, and sip it slowly."

Enjoy the journey. Your destination is not the most important thing, he says; the process of getting there is. "People often think, 'I'll be happy when I get there,' but usually that doesn't happen. It's important to have goals, but the most important thing is not arriving at the goal, but the enjoyment of the process of getting there."

{a beautiful mind}

Sleep and diet also play a crucial role in how your brain functions (see Part I). Sleep affects attention, memory, cognitive skills, and mood. Food affects the brain in many ways by releasing chemicals that influence mood. "There is more and more interest in the food and mood connection—I think we're going to hear a lot more about it in years to come," says Joan Borysenko, Ph.D., a psychologist and author of *Your Soul's Compass: What Is Spiritual Guidance?* and *Minding the Body, Mending the Mind*. "I think a lot of women who eat chocolate use it as an antidepressant, for example."

Overall tip: What's good for the heart is also good for the brain. Clear arteries mean that oxygen-rich blood will flow easily to your brain with no obstructions along the way. A brain-healthy diet should include foods high in antioxidants (such as leafy green vegetables and fruits like blueberries, which protect the brain from cell-damaging free radicals) and omega-3 fatty acids (such as salmon and tuna, which reduce inflammation in the body and keep arteries clear). ☕

{use it or lose it:
active mind, healthy mind}

As we get older, our cognitive skills—such as memory, attention, and reasoning—can decline if we don't make an effort to keep our minds stimulated through reading, learning new things, and engaging in challenging mental activities. Over the last decade—coinciding with the aging of forever-young baby boomers—there has been a keen interest in the subject of mental exercise. There are now many websites, programs, software, and books devoted to keeping the mind young and sharp, offering everything from games to exercises. Here are just a few:

• Positscience.com—Posit Science is the developer of the Brain Fitness Program, a software program that focuses on listening and communication skills; $395 for individuals; $495 for families; $595 with coaching kit.

• Happy-neuron.com—offers regular brain workouts for subscribers; monthly membership, $9.95; annual membership, $99.95. Each membership comes with a free seven-day trial.

- Sharpbrains.com—offers several brain exercise products, including software, DVDs, and books.

- Mybraintrainer.com—calling itself "the world's first and best virtual mental gymnasium," the site offers daily Braintraining sessions with cognitive exercises designed to stimulate the mind; $9.95 for 3 months.

- Gamesforthebrain.com—offers all kinds of games, from trivia quizzes to checkers.

- Brain Age: Train Your Brain in Minutes a Day— a video game played on a Nintendo DS handheld system; it's based on the brain exercises that were developed by the Japanese neuroscientist Dr. Ryuta Kawashima. ⬀

*S*PIRIT

III. THE JOURNEY INWARD: A HEALTHY SPIRIT

We are not human beings

having a spiritual experience.

We are spiritual beings having

a human experience.

—PIERRE TEILHARD DE CHARDIN

What is spirit? That depends on whom you ask. Some people see it as a mystical force that transcends the material world—call it the soul, God, Divine energy, the source, higher consciousness, or love. Some believe it is our true self, the essence of who we really are. Others think of it as that still, small voice they hear from time to time in dreams or through intuition. Some believe it is all those things and more.

Spirituality has been likened to a journey, an exploration of life's big questions: Who am I? Why am I here? What is the meaning of my existence?

There are many roads along the journey. Some of us find our way through religious faith; others find it through nature or meditation or service to others.

The majority of Americans consider themselves to be spiritual. According to a 2005 *Newsweek*/Beliefnet Poll, 79 percent (especially those under sixty years old) described themselves as spiritual. The poll also reported that almost two-thirds of Americans say they pray every day, and nearly a third meditate.

Some studies show that people with spiritual or religious

beliefs are more likely to have better health and to live longer than nonbelievers. Among other benefits, a strong belief system provides a sense of purpose in life, offers comfort in the face of personal trials or ill health, helps us handle the stresses of life, and eases isolation by giving us the sense that we are part of something greater than ourselves.

All of us have the potential to be spiritual. How can we get in touch with that deeper part of ourselves? In the following pages, several of the country's most esteemed experts offer their opinions about how to do it.

The essentials for living a spiritual life are:

A sense of oneness and connection

Time for reflection

A sense of awe and wonder

A sense of purpose

Meaningful ritual

In Harmony:
A Sense of Oneness and Connection

We are caught in an inescapable network of mutuality,
tied in a single garment of destiny. Whatever affects one
directly, affects all indirectly.

—REVEREND DR. MARTIN LUTHER KING, JR.

At the heart of every major religion is a common spiritual teaching: Treat others as you would like to be treated. In other words, put yourself in your neighbor's shoes and act accordingly. It is the Golden Rule, the foundation for ethics and morality. It is about feeling a deep connection with humanity as a whole and a sense of responsibility to help those in need—to "bear ye one another's burdens," as it says in the Bible. The point is, in spite of our diversity and differences, we are all part of the human family. The essentials for oneness and connection are:

Compassion for all living beings
Transcendence of self and healthy sense of self
The capacity to forgive others and ourselves
A sense of fellowship

Why We Need a Sense of Oneness and Connection

We are all social creatures, who need to be in relationship with others. Our survival depends on it: human connection is fundamental for physical and mental health. More and more evidence shows that people who have strong social networks—who feel a sense of emotional support—are healthier and happier, and live longer.

Human connection is also one of the foundations for spirituality. When we feel a sense of fellowship with others, we learn to transcend the self—by seeing that we are all one in spirit. The renowned Trappist monk Thomas Merton once said, "Love is our true destiny. We do not find the meaning of life by ourselves alone—we find it with another." When we feel a sense of oneness with others, when we identify with their needs or suffering, we find the true meaning of love and compassion—and feel closer to Divine presence.

"One of the main goals of every spiritual tradition I know is that there's a need for people to go beyond the self, to have an awareness that there is something larger, more powerful, and wiser than ourselves," says Dr. Larry Dossey, author of *Healing Words* and *The Extraordinary Healing Power of Ordinary Things: Fourteen Natural Steps to Health and Happiness.* "As Ravi Ravindra, a teacher and author, put it, 'Spirituality is not about freedom for yourself, it is about freedom from yourself.' This is echoed in every major religion, all of which have some sort of Golden Rule that emphasizes love, compassion, and identifying with the needs of others."

Essentials: What the Experts Say

Feeling a sense of oneness and connection with others—and with ourselves—is a fundamental part of the spiritual journey. The essentials are:

Compassion for all living beings. Compassion is the cornerstone of love and ethics. It is the ability to understand and identify with the plight of other living beings and have a sense of responsibility to alleviate their suffering through acts of kindness and generosity.

Compassion does not only extend to the people we love but also to the entire human family. At its core is the belief that we are all one in spirit. "Never forget that every human being is fashioned in the image of God," says Rabbi Harold S. Kushner, author of *Overcoming Life's Disappointments* and *Living a Life That Matters*. "That means unsuccessful people, annoying people, physically and mentally disabled people, very young and very old people—every single one of them is a bearer of the image of God."

Having this awareness brings us closer to the Divine. "When you really come to genuinely care and empathize with people, you realize a sense of unity or oneness with them," says Dr. Dossey. "At a certain stage you aren't just doing good or being nice to other people. What you're doing is empathizing and being compassionate toward yourself because you so totally identify with the rest of the world that there's no difference, there's no barrier. For people who really get it, it's an abiding certainty that you're in it with everybody else, you're not separate from them."

A key element in being compassionate is giving back through service to others. "Spirituality is personal and public, you can't separate the two," says Reverend Otis Moss III, pastor of Trinity United Church of Christ in Chicago, and a regular guest on the Naomi Judd *New Morning Show* on the Hallmark Channel. "You cannot have love without compassion—identifying with others' pain and seeing yourself as connected to their personal struggle. How do you express that? How do you live that? Through service to others in your community. Through service, you connect to the holy."

Transcendence of self and healthy sense of self. This statement may seem contradictory, but it is not. "The basic principle of all legitimate wisdom traditions is to transcend one's self, or ego," says Dr. Dossey. Transcendence means getting closer to our deeper self by letting go of obstacles that hinder spiritual development—conceit, materialism, greed, and the quest for power and perfectionism, for example. At the same time, the Golden Rule tells us to love ourselves as well as our neighbor. Loving ourselves is not self-centeredness. It is about accepting who we are—our strengths as well as our weaknesses—and believing we are lovable and worthy beings.

"A mature sense of self is absolutely necessary to progress on the spiritual path," says Dr. Dossey. "As the saying goes, 'In order to transcend the self, you first have to have one.' There's a tremendous amount of wisdom in that. You have to have a sense of yourself as a worthy individual." For many of us—particularly women, who tend to be the nurturers of others—it sometimes is easier to love and care for other people than it is ourselves. But we need to remember that we, too, are made in the image of God, and the same compassion, forgiveness, and kindness that we show to others must also be shown to ourselves.

"Included in this world is an extremely precious and important person, who is you, who must be tended to as well," says Elizabeth Gilbert, author of *Eat, Pray, Love: One Woman's Search for Everything Across Italy, India and Indonesia* and *Pilgrims*. "I'm not saying neglect the soup kitchen, but there are often times when you will find there is a part of you that's standing there with an empty bowl."

The capacity to forgive others and ourselves. When we have been hurt or wronged by someone—whether a family member, a friend, a spouse, or a stranger—it can be very difficult to handle residual feelings of anger, hatred, bitterness, or revenge. These powerful feelings can impede our spiritual life, cutting us off from love and connection.

But deep wounds take time to heal—and recovery may require getting professional or religious counseling. The reason: Holding on to these powerful negative emotions can be poisonous, not only to our spirit but, according to research, to the health of our mind and body as well.

Forgiveness is the willingness to let go of resentments and hostilities toward another for wrongdoings. It may create a path toward reconciliation, yet it may not: sometimes other people do not acknowledge or take responsibility for their offense. That doesn't matter. Forgiveness offers us release, the chance to overcome emotional turmoil, to heal and move on. Of course, it isn't an easy process; we have to be ready.

"When someone hurts us deeply, it can take a long time to process the feelings and release the person from feelings of revenge or retaliation," says Dr. Arthur Caliandro, senior minister at Marble Collegiate Church in New York City and author of *Simple Steps: 10 Things You Can Do to Create an Exceptional Life* and *Make Your Life Count*. "But when we forgive, we are free, free from the negative hold the other person has on us." But we may need help in doing that, he says. "I do not believe that for the big injuries of life we can forgive by ourselves. We need the intercession and participation of God."

Nearly all the world's major spiritual traditions teach forgiveness. "It is at the very center of the Christian faith," says Dr. Caliandro. "If Jesus had not forgiven those who took his life, there would have been no resurrection. He needed to be clear and pure in his attitude toward others."

When we cannot let go of these negative emotions, they will eventually take their toll on us. "Holding on to anger is like grasping a hot coal with the intent of throwing it at someone else, but you are the one who gets burned," says the Buddha.

"When you cannot forgive, you end up carrying around a whole lot of baggage that keeps you from growing into your full human potential," says Reverend Moss. "You're giving power to someone else by giving them the ability to disrupt your life. Forgiveness allows you to see the situation in a different way by changing the frame of the picture. Forgiveness is more for you than for the other person. It frees you up, it releases you, and liberates your spirit."

Holding on to old wounds—sometimes for centuries—is at the heart of many world conflicts, says Dr. Dossey. "Think what happens when people can't forgive and forget. Bosnia remembered its defeat at the Battle of Kosovo in the fourteenth century, and the ongoing hatred played a role in the war there. And Germany could not forget its defeat and humiliation in World War I, which led directly to World War II. Would the world not have been better if some forgiving had taken place in each instance?"

How do we go about forgiving? "It doesn't mean becoming amnesiac for wrongs and slights from others, but forgetting in the sense that the memory does not trigger anger, hostility, aggression, and the negative impact on our mental and physical health that goes with these negative emotions," says Dr. Dossey. "This happens when we learn how to replace anger, hostility, and hatred with tolerance, empathy, and love."

The process of forgiveness extends also to ourselves. For years people can hold on to feelings of guilt, anger, hatred, and shame—for their own past wrongs toward others or their own mistakes or failures. You have to offer yourself the same forgiveness that you extend to others.

A sense of fellowship. Being part of a group of like-minded souls gives us a sense of community or belonging, a feeling that we are part of something greater than ourselves. Many religious traditions believe that being with other believers—participating in communal worship in a church, synagogue, or mosque—connects us to one another and to Divine presence.

"God is accessible at all times and by many paths, but it's a lot easier to find God in the company of other searchers," says Rabbi Kushner. "People need community. That might be the most valuable thing religious involvement does for the nourishment of the soul—provide us with community."

Of course, you don't have to be a member of a religious community to feel a sense of fellowship with others. You can join a meditation or prayer group or attend spiritual or nature retreats. If you don't want to be part of a group, you can serve your community by volunteering at a local hospital, homeless shelter, or charity, delivering meals to the elderly, teaching a child to read, cleaning up parks, or painting a local school. (See "Work That Feeds the Soul," page 331.)

{the golden rule by any other name}

Almost all of the world's major religions share a common teaching: to treat others as we would like to be treated. Here are some quotes from a variety of faiths:

Judaism: "Thou shalt not take vengeance, nor bear any grudge against the children of thy people; but thou shalt love thy neighbor as thyself: I am Jehovah."—LEVITICUS 19:18

Buddhism: "Hurt not others in ways that you yourself would find harmful."—UDANAVARGA 5,1

Christianity: "All things therefore whatsoever ye would that men should do unto you, even so do ye also unto them: for this is the law and the prophets."—MATTHEW 7:12

Hinduism: "This is the sum of duty; do naught onto others what you would not have them do unto you."—MAHABHARATA 5,1517

Confucianism: "Do not do to others what you would not like yourself. Then there will be no resentment against you, either in the family or in the state."—ANALECTS 12 : 2

Islam: "No one of you is a believer until he desires for his brother that which he desires for himself."—SUNNAH 🛡

Sources: American Standard Version of the Holy Bible, and www .religioustolerance.org

{work that feeds the soul}

Did you know that more than 65.4 million Americans volunteer? One of the best ways to get outside your world is to focus on the needs of someone who is needier than you are. By helping others you help yourself—because the giver actually gets more in return.

There are many ways to open your heart—whether it's helping disaster victims, reading to the blind, or teaching English as a second language. Whatever your area of interest is, you can find thousands of volunteer opportunities in this country and all over the world. It's as simple as going to a website—here are some great ones to check out:

Volunteermatch.org—This San Francisco–based nonprofit group works with about 50,000 organizations, offering service opportunities all over the United States, in areas including advocacy and human rights, hurricane relief, women's issues, and immigrants and refugees.

Volunteersolutions.org—Operated by United Way charities, this organization works with about 45,000 agencies, offering service opportunities from A to Z all over the United States, in areas including animals, the environment, and the homeless.

USAfreedomcorps.gov—This is the site of a government agency created after 9/11 to promote service. It will link you with many opportunities (and government agencies like Senior Corps, Americorps, and Citizen Corps) all over the United States, in areas including public safety, hurricane relief, and human services.

Networkforgood.org—Founded in 2001 by America Online, Cisco Systems, and Yahoo!, this nonprofit organization offers 36,000 volunteer opportunities all over the United States, in areas including education, public safety, and crisis relief. (You can also donate to your favorite cause on this site.)

Volunteer.gov—This is a government site providing opportunities in the public sector—including working with the National Park Service, the U.S. Department of Veterans Affairs, and the U.S. Geological Survey.

Goabroad.com—An alternative travel resource that lists A to Z volunteer opportunities (from academic reinforcement to youth ministry) all over the world, including Peru, Thailand, Nepal, and Ghana.

Volunteerinternational.org—Run by the International Volunteer Programs Association, a nonprofit alliance, this site features links to organizations around the world that offer volunteer opportunities.

Globalvolunteers.org—This site, run by a non-profit group in St. Paul, Minnesota, offers service opportunities from A to Z (from teaching conversational English to painting community buildings).

Habitat.org—This is the site for Habitat for Humanity International, a nonprofit ministry founded in 1976 that builds shelter for the needy—to date, they have built more than 225,000 homes. Habitat offers volunteer opportunities all over the United States and abroad, including countries in Africa, the Middle East, Asia, and Latin America.

Handsonnetwork.org—This nonprofit organization, based in Atlanta, Georgia, is made up of fifty-eight national and international volunteer organizations that offer a vast range of community-based projects—including working in disaster recovery, homeless shelters, food banks, senior centers, and community green spaces.

Peacecorps.org—This government agency, founded in 1960 by John F. Kennedy, offers all types of volunteer opportunities in developing countries around the globe, including education, youth outreach and community development, business development, agriculture and environment, health and HIV/AIDS, and information technology. Since its founding, more than 187,000 Americans have served in more than 139 countries around the world. ☺

Still Water: Time for Reflection

In the attitude of silence the soul finds the path in a clearer
light, and what is elusive and deceptive resolves itself
into crystal clearness.

—MAHATMA GANDHI

One of the most valuable commodities of modern life is
time. We live by the clock—juggling the demands of work,
family, and running a household. With so many responsibilities and distractions (television, computers, BlackBerries,
and cell phones, to name a few), it can be difficult to find
time to devote to our spiritual side. Often the still, small
voice can't be heard amid the din of mind chatter, with
its worries and concerns. But the voice is there. To hear it
more clearly, we must be quiet and listen. The essentials for
reflection are:

Meditation, prayer, or contemplation
Reading
Writing or other creative pursuits

Why We Need Time for Reflection

We are more than just our bodies. We also are spiritual beings who long to understand fundamental questions about the
purpose and meaning of our existence. Most humans, even if
some are not consciously aware of it, yearn to connect with
something deeper—call it the soul, the source, or the Divine.
Whatever you call it, it dwells within each of us. As the writer
Hermann Hesse said, "Within you there is a stillness and a sanctuary to which you can retreat at any time and be yourself."

Finding that still, small voice isn't easy in today's hectic
world. Some people can spend a lifetime without ever hearing it, or some avoid hearing it because the process of listening may bring up uncomfortable feelings.

"The voice is pushed down by the competing voices of
all the things that people have to do. And every year those
lists seem to get longer and longer," says Elizabeth Gilbert,
author of *Eat, Pray, Love: One Woman's Search for Everything
Across Italy, India and Indonesia* and *Pilgrims*.

But in order to connect with ourselves and spiritual energy, we must step back, be quiet, and listen. "You need time

when you are not in action, when your attention is not being diverted away from yourself," says Gilbert. "There is a Zen expression that says you cannot see your reflection in moving water, only in still water."

When we take time to reflect, we tune out the distractions that can cloud our minds. We have more clarity.

"Taking time to reflect is one of the keys to spirituality," says Dr. Arthur Caliandro, senior minister at Marble Collegiate Church in New York and author of *Simple Steps: 10 Things You Can Do to Create an Exceptional Life* and *Make Your Life Count*. "There is power in quiet moments. It's been said that music is the silence between the notes. And God is found in the pauses, in the silences."

Stillness—whether we find it in prayer or meditation or walk in the woods—allows us greater receptivity to the Divine.

Essentials: What the Experts Say

To become more reflective, the essentials are:

Meditation, prayer, or contemplation. Sometimes we have to close our eyes in order to see. To be reflective doesn't mean living in solitude or joining a monastery. It can mean just taking a few minutes out of our day to stop and connect with ourselves. One of the best ways to do that is through quiet pursuits like meditation, prayer, or mindful contemplation. When we are still, we are relaxed and therefore in a receptive frame of mind.

"Of course, God exists everywhere, but it's when you carve out time from the world that you notice and can respond," says Gilbert. "The early mystics said that prayer was a lute string that attached humanity to the Divine. When you pluck on one end of it, there's a vibrational response on the other end. And it works in the other direction as well. When the Divine is trying to communicate with you, there's a reverb on that lute string. But if you don't have the time and space in which to receive the vibration, you won't feel it."

"Whether you call it meditation, contemplation, or prayer, there is a time when you need to sit down and be quiet and listen," says Dr. Larry Dossey, author of *Healing Words* and *The Extraordinary Healing Power of Ordinary Things: Fourteen Natural Steps to Health and Happiness*. "But it doesn't have to be any far-out, esoteric behavior."

For instance, communing with nature—hiking in the woods, walking on a beach or even in a city park—can be a contemplative experience and can take us to a higher place. "Nature opens the heart and reveals the preciousness of the world," Dr. Dossey says.

Reading. Another aspect of being reflective is to expand your mind through intelligent study. If you are interested in spirituality, you need to learn as much about it as you can. This includes reading religious texts as well as inspirational literature.

"I've learned that most of my spirituality has been developed through study," says Thomas Moore, author of *Care of the Soul: A Guide for Cultivating Depth and Sacredness in Everyday Life* and *The Soul's Religion: Cultivating a Profoundly Spiritual Way of Life.* "So for me that means studying the world's religious traditions. It isn't enough for someone to say 'I'm going to develop a spiritual life' and then pick up the latest pop spirituality book. The best thing is to read the classic texts like the *Tao Te Ching* of China, the Buddhist sutras, the great poems from the Sufi tradition, the great Christian mystics, or the great Jewish commentaries in the Old Testament. So I would say become intelligent about spirituality through study because so much of what we see, if I can say it, is just dumb."

Other types of literature, like poetry or biographies of outstanding people, for instance, also elevate the spirit. "I'm a voracious reader," says Dr. Dossey. "When I read about the lives of people who have managed to achieve and transcend, I find that immensely inspiring in my own life."

Writing or other creative pursuits. Getting in touch with our creative energy can be one of the highest forms of self-reflection. The discipline of daily writing—keeping a journal—is a great way to connect with ourselves. "Anything you can do to practice intimacy with yourself is useful, and journaling is something I've done throughout my life," says Gilbert. "I think an active journal, one in which you continually pose the questions, 'Who am I, what am I here for, what is my purpose?'—and try very hard to answer those questions—will help open doors for you."

She adds, "I never noticed until now the similarity of the words *journal* and *journey*—they must share a root. I see the journal as a kind of expedition both inward and outward."

If you do keep a journal, try to write it the old-fashioned way: pen to paper. In her book *The Vein of Gold*, author Julia Cameron writes, "We are on a pilgrimage, and writing by hand allows us to examine more closely the journey we are taking."

Other creative pursuits—like listening to or playing music, painting, drawing, or whatever area of the arts that interests you—can stir the soul and take you out of yourself and to a more spiritual place. "I just wish people would give themselves permission to discover the treasures that are hidden within them and to believe that that is a worthy way to spend a little of their time while living, because I think that's the closest we can get to the Divine on earth," says Gilbert.

{getaways for the soul}

The idea of spiritual retreat—being in a sacred place where we can reflect, pray, or meditate in silence as part of a community, without the distractions of the world—is a common practice in many religious traditions. A time out for your soul can be a wonderful way to deepen your spirituality. How do you find a place that's right for you? Here are some websites to get you started:

Findthedivine.com

Journeysofthespirit.com

Nardacenters.org

Retreatfinder.com

Retreatsintl.org

Seekaretreat.com

Spiritsite.com

Profound Reverence:
A Sense of Awe and Wonder

There are two ways to live your life. One is as though nothing
is a miracle, the other is as though everything is a miracle.

—ALBERT EINSTEIN

There's no denying the fact that life is full of responsibilities and pressures. But sometimes we become so limited in our view of the world that we lose sight of the majesty that surrounds us. We forget to be amazed by a flower growing, the sun rising, or our own heart beating. But once in a while we have one of those crystal moments when we realize how astonishing it all is. For me, it's those summer nights on the beach in Amagansett, New York, when I'm looking up at the stars. We must hold on to those moments, because they inspire in us a sense of awe and wonder, which is one of the pathways to the Divine. The essentials for awe and wonder are:

A deep appreciation of nature and the world
A sense of reverence for life
An attitude of openness
A feeling of gratitude

Why We Need Awe and Wonder

Awe is a feeling of amazement (sometimes even fear) inspired by witnessing something truly sublime or magnificent. One universal inspiration for awe is nature—in its unparalleled beauty, variety, and mysteriousness as well as its fierce power (witness the destructive force of volcanoes, storms, earthquakes, tsunamis, and so on).

Having a sense of awe and wonder is essential to spirituality, because it reminds us that there is something bigger than ourselves. Awe is humbling.

"When we look at all the intricacies of creation—human beings, the solar system, our ecosystem, the micro-universe of cells and atoms—it's pretty awe-inspiring," says the Reverend Otis Moss III, pastor of Trinity United Church of Christ in Chicago and a regular guest on the Naomi Judd *New Morning Show* on the Hallmark Channel. "We see something greater than ourselves. It gives us a sense of humility."

One of the downsides of modern living is that many people have limited contact with the cycle of nature. The majority of us live in or near urban areas—we don't see the sun rise or set and we cannot see the stars because city light shrouds them.

We can become so self-involved that we lose awareness of the magic that surrounds us. When Rabbi Harold S. Kushner, author of *Overcoming Life's Disappointments* and *Living a Life That Matters,* was a student at the Jewish Theological Seminary in New York City, one of his teachers was the renowned theologian Abraham Joshua Heschel, who wrote extensively about the importance of awe and wonder in relationship to the Divine. "His [Heschel's] enduring message was that the religious soul really starts with a sense of wonder and awe, and if we ever lose that, real spirituality probably is impossible," says Rabbi Kushner. "I remember one evening he came into class and said, 'A remarkable thing happened as I was coming to class.' And we all perked up and said, 'What was it?' And he answered, 'The sun set. The sun set and nobody on Broadway noticed it.'"

Finding the time to notice the mysteries and wonders around us can be difficult in a fast-paced highly technological society. "This is a culture that's all about productivity," says Elizabeth Gilbert, author of *Eat, Pray, Love: One Woman's Search for Everything Across Italy, India and Indonesia* and *Pilgrims.* "And I'm not a critic of that because there are fantastic things about it. As someone who's lived in cultures where there is no such thing, there's a lot to be said for productivity. But it does come at a cost, and the cost is the idea of stillness."

In a society that is constantly in motion, it can be difficult to stop and take notice. Doing too much and having too much can be numbing to the spirit. We begin to take things for granted. Yet mysteries are all around us—we just have to take the time to look with a renewed vision.

"Anything that gets you in touch with the mysteriousness of the world is essential to spiritual life," says Thomas Moore, the author of *Care of the Soul: A Guide for Cultivating Depth and Sacredness in Everyday Life* and *The Soul's Religion: Cultivating a Profoundly Spiritual Way of Life*. "We have a problem today because science wants to explain everything. And we have to resist that tendency to be totally scientific. We can be sophisticated in our science but at the same time cultivate a sense of awe about nature and not feel compelled to explain it all or that we have to accept every explanation."

Essentials: What the Experts Say

How do you cultivate awe and wonder? It's simple: Stop, look, and listen. In other words, be still, pay attention, and tune in to the world in a new way. The essentials are:

A deep appreciation of nature and the world. At some point in our lives most of us ask: How did all of this come to be? The beauty of the earth, the air we breathe, the intricate design of a snowflake, the vastness of space—everything in this universe, from the smallest to the largest, inspires wonder. If you're afflicted with world-weariness, just think about this: We are just one planet in a galaxy among hundreds of billions of other galaxies; that fact alone is truly mind-boggling.

"It is an amazing show," says Elizabeth Gilbert. "Sometimes I just watch pigeons fly and I think, 'What if I had never seen a bird and then all of a sudden I saw one?' It would be the most amazing, miraculous thing. And yet, we just don't see it. I think it comes back to time and stillness, being able to take a moment and look around and be in wonder."

To awaken that sense of wonder, we have to try to see the world as though it were for the first time, to experience it as children do. "When we're kids, in particular, the world seems so awesome," says Dr. Arthur Caliandro, senior minister of Marble Collegiate Church in New York City and the author of *Simple Steps: 10 Things You Can Do to Create an Exceptional Life* and *Make Your Life Count.* "When we are adults we have to continue to cultivate that wonder and allow ourselves to be awed, because it places us in a spiritual dimension."

A sense of reverence for life. "By having a reverence for life, we enter into a spiritual relation with the world," said the humanitarian and Nobel Peace Prize winner Dr. Albert Schweitzer. "By practicing reverence for life we become good, deep, and alive."

Reverence is a profound appreciation for the miracle and mystery of life itself. You can start practicing by seeing the wonder in yourself and other human beings: The fact that you exist. The fact that you are a marvel of creation: that your heart beats 100,000 times a day and you breathe about 40 million breaths a year; that your body is made up of a complex group of systems that all work together; that you are mind, body, and spirit.

"You have to have self-awe," says Gilbert. "Not necessarily because I am me but because I merely am. Carried within you in your very being is a wellspring of phenomenal wonder, the fact that you exist. Just merely being is absolutely miraculous. What a thing life is!"

An attitude of openness. To have awe and wonder requires openness of mind—that is, a sense of curiosity and an awareness that there are no absolutes, that there are still many new things to learn, no matter how old or educated we are. Openness is the opposite of smugness or arrogance. "It means being open to the mysteriousness of the world around you," says Moore. "You cannot think you know everything and be a spiritual person." He speaks of his book *The Soul's Religion: Cultivating a Profoundly Spiritual Way of Life*. "I opened it with images of emptiness, like the Pantheon in Rome, most of which is an empty space. There is no roof. So if it rains when you're in the temple, then you get rained on. That's an image for openness of mind. It's an attitude of being open to life as it comes and open to the variety of life as it appears."

A feeling of gratitude. Abundance and beauty surround us—in nature and in our personal lives—but sometimes we fail to notice. When we take things for granted, we develop a sense of entitlement: we become world-weary and jaded— the exact opposite of feeling awe and wonder. But when we acknowledge and appreciate all that we have—the air we breathe; the people in our lives; our food, our home, our work, and so on—it makes us more open to receiving life's blessings and ultimately brings us closer to Divine presence. A grateful heart helps us view the world anew.

"I think gratitude is a natural offshoot of wonder." says Elizabeth Gilbert. "I've made a practice in my own life that every night before I go to bed, I take thirty seconds to say this is a wonder, a wonder—everything—from the fact that I have a roof over my head to the fact that I'm breathing this oxygen and living—I say thank you for that. And now I'm going to disappear into sleep, which is another wonder."

Gratitude should be practiced as a kind of spiritual discipline, like prayer, experts say.

"It links with prayer and meditation," says Dr. Larry Dossey, author of *Healing Words* and *The Extraordinary Healing Power of Ordinary Things: Fourteen Natural Steps to Health and Happiness*. "Every morning when I put my feet on the floor I say a little prayer of gratitude. And it's become inconceivable to me that I could eat a meal and not silently say a few words of gratitude."

Acknowledging blessings makes us receptive to other blessings. "Everyone has pain and problems," says Dr. Caliandro. "But in this country we are so blessed, our cup runneth over, and we need to acknowledge that every day when we get up in the morning, even if we feel bad."

{awesome fast facts}

Do you feel a lack of awe in your life? Here are just a few of the many wonders about the world:

• There are an estimated 100 billion stars in our galaxy, the Milky Way, and there are an estimated (no one really knows) 500 billion galaxies in the universe.

• Each snowflake is unique.

• The human foot, a wonder of engineering, has fifty-six bones and two hundred ligaments.

• There are an estimated 10 quintillion (a number with 18 zeroes) insects in the world but only a million or more have been identified.

• The blue whale is the largest animal on earth—some can weigh as much as 300,000 pounds.

• Your heart beats about 100,000 times a day and 40 million times a year.

• Our brains have more than 100 million nerve cells. ⬧

{ways to open the heart}

• Express gratitude every day either in prayer or meditation.

• Volunteer a few hours a week through a local hospital, church, synagogue, or charitable organization to help someone less fortunate.

• Do activities that elevate the spirit—try to spend time in nature, read inspirational literature, listen to beautiful music, or visit a museum.

• Join a community of like-minded seekers—such as a church or meditation group.

• Create sacred space or an altar in your home for prayer, meditation, or quiet contemplation.

• Practice acts of kindness, compassion, and forgiveness. ☞

{words to live by every day}

How can you become more spiritual? Start your day with inspirational quotations and affirmations. Here are some websites that provide daily words of inspiration:

Actsofkindness.org

Dailygood.org

Dailyguideposts.com

DailyOM.com

Dailyword.com

Dailyzen.com

Gratefulness.org

Inner Compass: A Sense of Purpose

A man without a purpose is like a ship
without a rudder.

—THOMAS CARLYLE

Who am I? Why am I here? Where am I going? We are all searching for answers to these questions in our spiritual journey. Some of us know early on where we're headed, while others never seem to find the right road. We can have all the trappings of money and success and think "Is that all there is?" When we have a sense of purpose, it gives our life meaning. It is a blueprint for being all that we are meant to be. It is about finding our truth. The essentials for a sense of purpose are:

A belief that your life has meaning

A belief that you are carrying out your purpose

Why We Need a Sense of Purpose

Most of us wouldn't dream of driving to a new destination without consulting a road map or a navigation system. So why would we live our lives not knowing where we're going? In some ways a sense of purpose is like an inner road map or navigation system, but it is even more than that. It's knowing where you're going and knowing why you're going there. It's the stuff that makes life worth living.

Each one of us has a unique and higher calling.

"There's a reason for everyone to be here," says Dr. Arthur Caliandro, senior minister of Marble Collegiate Church in New York City and the author of *Simple Steps: 10 Things You Can Do to Create an Exceptional Life* and *Make Your Life Count*. "One of the spiritual challenges is finding meaning. When a person finds meaning, they find their truth. It's a very spiritual experience. I'm not speaking from a religious standpoint because religion gets tied into institutions. I'm speaking about who we are as human beings and we are souls."

Dr. Caliandro speaks about Pierre Teilhard de Chardin, a French Jesuit priest who was a mystic and a scientist. "Chardin was a seeker of the truth. He said, 'We are not human beings having a spiritual experience. We are spiritual beings having a human experience.' What does that mean? We are here for a very short period of time. Within the eons of history, we're little tiny dots on the spectrum. We come from a spiritual place and return to a spiritual place."

When we connect to our spiritual "place," we begin to see our lives in a different way. We realize that we are part of something greater—that our sense of purpose is found above and beyond ourselves, in the things that feed our souls and make us feel closer to Divine spirit.

Essentials: What the Experts Say

Having a sense of purpose is an integral part of spirituality. The essentials are:

A belief that your life has meaning. This is linked to an age-old question: Why am I here? We all want to feel that we are in this world for some reason, that we matter, and that our lives have value. "Everyone wants his or her life to count for something," says Dr. Caliandro. "We all want our lives to have meaning."

How do we find meaning? That is the challenge of everyone's journey, and of course, one size does not fit all. But, experts say, look to the simple things that give us a sense of joy and connect us to Divine spirit: prayer or meditation; giving service to others; relationships with family, friends, and community; appreciation of nature; rewarding work.

Meaning lies in the things that nourish our souls, not our vanity. "In America we don't take time to reflect much on the real values that make life worth living," says the Reverend Otis Moss III, pastor of Trinity United Church of Christ in Chicago and a regular guest on the Naomi Judd *New Morning Show* on the Hallmark Channel. "We think more about 'how am I going to get something on an external level that shows I have purpose—a larger car, a bigger house, or expensive clothes?' "

Having a purpose doesn't mean we have to save the world. "The problem is some of us think that we have to have this incredibly grand scheme like 'I'm going to stop the violence in the Middle East,' " says Reverend Moss. "But a sense of purpose could be something very simple—it could be the gift of encouraging other people or caring for your grandmother or being a loving parent to your children. It could be anything where you know you are allowing God's hand to guide you, to bring love into the world."

A belief that you are carrying out your purpose. Having a sense of purpose is one of the cornerstones of a spiritual life.

We all need to feel that we are valued members of society and that we are making a contribution in some way.

"I think that every human being for the full development of the soul needs to have a sense that he or she has made a difference to the world, that the world is in some large or small way a better place for you having passed through it," says Rabbi Harold S. Kushner, the author of *Overcoming Life's Disappointments* and *Living a Life That Matters*. "It's having a sense of purpose and the successful carrying out of that purpose."

Making a difference often can mean having to change your life, which may require courage and perhaps taking some risks. For instance, if you have a successful yet unfulfilling career as a lawyer but have always wanted to teach impoverished children in a developing country, you will have to take a significant leap to do that.

Of course, making a difference doesn't always pertain to your career. It can also be challenging yourself in some way outside your comfort zone.

"You have to permit yourself to become uncomfortable," says Dr. Larry Dossey, the author of *Healing Words* and *The Extraordinary Healing Power of Ordinary Things: Fourteen Steps to Health and Happiness*. "It's easy to stay in habits, ruts, and routines. I'm talking about going somewhere where you've never been before, like taking a stand on an issue."

And today there are more than enough issues to take a stand on. "Embrace the world with caring and compassion," says Dr. Dossey. "This is more than a nice phrase; these days it's a matter of some urgency. When the fate of our planet may be at stake from environmental degradation, global climate change, overpopulation, and wars spawned by a thousand hatreds, a world-embracing effort is more critical than ever before if we are to survive."

{the daily grind}

Nothing withers the spirit more than getting up every morning and going to a job that you despise. Unfortunately, many of us are doing just that. Over the last twenty years job satisfaction in America has been on the decline among people of all ages and income levels, reported the Conference Board, a worldwide business research group. According to a 2006 survey by the group, less than half of all Americans say they like their jobs, compared with 61 percent in 1987; the survey found that the least satisfied were young people under twenty-five. ☁

{god: male or female?}

Who or what is God? Here are some fascinating findings from a 2006 Harris Poll:

• Seventy-three percent of Americans believe in God, but only 58 percent are "absolutely certain" there is a God.

• Six percent do not believe in God.

• Seventy-three percent of Republicans are "absolutely certain" there is a God, while only 58 percent of Democrats have that certainty.

• Thirty-six percent of Americans think God is male and one percent think God is female.

• Forty-one percent think God is a spirit or power that can take on human form but is not inherently human.

• Nine percent think God has a human form.

• Forty-four percent believe that God observes but does not control what happens on Earth.

Source: The Harris Poll® #80, October 31, 2006

{who's happy?}

Americans are, that's who. A recent Harris poll found that a startling 94 percent of us are satisfied with our lives. The survey said that 56 percent said they were very satisfied and 38 percent said they were somewhat satisfied.

Though there was overall life satisfaction across all age groups, older Americans (sixty-two years and over) were more content than younger generations (eighteen to thirty years old). Regions of the country differed in their responses: 60 percent of southerners and 62 percent of westerners felt that their lives had improved over the last five years, compared with just 42 percent of easterners.

As far as the future, three out of five Americans think their lives will get better in the next five years. Again, regions of the country differed in their optimism: 68 percent of westerners expect their lives to get better while 56 percent of easterners shared that belief. ☞

Source: The Harris Poll® #80, August 14, 2007

Sacred Reminder: Meaningful Ritual

*Your sacred space is where you can find
yourself again and again.*

—JOSEPH CAMPBELL

To many people the word *ritual* conjures images of magic spells or spooky dances performed by the light of the moon. Truth is, every culture has rituals, and we all participate in them. They are reminders of meaningful events. For example, there are rituals to honor major passages in our lives—marriage, birth, and death. There are holiday rituals—watching the ball drop in Times Square on New Year's Eve or decorating the Christmas tree are just a few. There are also daily rituals and family rituals. Ritual connects us.

Many religions use ritual—generally in ceremonies with prayers or music—to remind us of our connection to God. But, no matter what your beliefs are, you can create your own spiritual rituals. They do not have to be elaborate—they can be simple, heartfelt words you write yourself. The essentials for meaningful ritual are:

  Any prayer, meditation, or activity that deepens spiritual connection

  A sacred space in your home

Why We Need Ritual

Rituals are symbolic acts—they serve as reminders of something meaningful to us. For instance, the rituals associated with baptisms, weddings, or funerals help us honor the change from one kind of life to another. And the rituals linked with certain holidays—even though the holidays may be spiritual in nature—remind us of connection to friends and family as well as our past.

"Rituals are about meaning," says the Reverend Otis Moss III, pastor of Trinity United Church of Christ in Chicago and a regular guest on the Naomi Judd *New Morning Show* on the Hallmark Channel. "Whether they are rituals of faith or rituals of community, I firmly believe that having these symbols in our lives in a consistent way is incredibly important because they elevate the human spirit."

Spiritual rituals remind us of our relationship with the Divine. Their purpose is to shift our thinking to a higher place, where we will be more open and receptive to spirit. But, to be effective, they must be done with intention. Any ritual done thoughtlessly or by rote renders it meaningless.

"I define ritual as any act that addresses the life of the soul," says Thomas Moore, author of *Care of the Soul: A Guide for Cultivating Depth and Sacredness in Everyday Life* and *The Soul's Religion*. "I think ritual is very important, but it has to be appreciated and done carefully. Just going to church every Sunday, while it may have value, can often become empty in a bad sense so that nothing happens."

A spiritual ritual must mean something to you. It can just be a simple thing—like saying a quiet prayer of gratitude when you awake every morning—but it should be done with thought. A ritual can involve gesture, language, objects, and images, whatever has meaning to you.

"There are all kinds of rituals—blessing your food before you eat is a simple ritual. It's a simple ritual that gives an atmosphere of spirituality to a home and a family," says Moore. "You need some concrete sign that you're thinking, that your attitude is spiritual—it doesn't happen automatically."

Essentials: What the Experts Say

Rituals don't have to be elaborate ceremonies or events.

They can be "any act that addresses the life of the soul," as Thomas Moore says. The essentials for rituals are:

Any prayer, meditation, or activity that deepens spiritual connection. A ritual can be anything that helps you connect with spirit: prayer (traditional prayers or those you create yourself), meditation, contemplation, chanting, or singing—even writing can be a form of ritual. You can write your own words for rituals for any number of reasons: gratitude, forgiveness, healing. As part of a ritual, you can also incorporate objects and things that set a contemplative mood: lighting candles, burning incense, ringing chimes or bells, playing beautiful music, or placing meaningful objects or images near you.

The only requirement is that the words and the act have meaning to you. "You can do almost anything if it affects you in a deep way," says Moore.

A spiritual ritual is your sacred time. When or how often you do it is up to you, of course. Some people find it helpful to set aside a certain time period. In fact, many religions have prayers for specific times of the day. For instance, Roman Catholics (and some Christian denominations) say the Angelus three times a day, usually at six in the morning, at noon, and at six in the evening, and Muslims are required to say

Salat, which are daily prayers recited five times during the day—dawn to sunrise, right after sunrise, midday, the late part of the afternoon, and between sunset and midnight.

Having a set time for your ritual may help you switch gears from a worldly dimension to a more spiritual one. It is likelier to become a habit that says: This is my time to stop and connect with self and spirit.

"If you set aside time and a place in your home for a ritual of meditation or prayer, you're more likely to engage in the ritual than winging it on a daily basis," says Dr. Larry Dossey, author of *Healing Word* and *The Extraordinary Power of Ordinary Things: Fourteen Steps to Health and Happiness.* "It becomes part of your daily affairs. So when the clock rolls around to a certain hour you know that that becomes your sacred time, a time you step aside and drop out of the mad race."

But a set time or place may not work for you. One thing you don't want is to think of spiritual ritual as drudgery, or something else you must do. "Sometimes I think people think, 'Oh, God, in addition to everything else now I have to meditate,'" says Elizabeth Gilbert, author of *Eat, Pray, Love: One Woman's Search for Everything Across Italy, India and Indonesia* and *Pilgrims.* Remember, your ritual can be what you want it to be. "Some days my spiritual practice is 'I'm going to take a nice walk.'"

A sacred space in your home. The best way to renew spiritual rituals is to create a sacred space in your home—a place set aside specifically to connect with self and spirit. A sacred space should be a calm sanctuary. It could be an altar of some kind, an entire room, or even a quiet corner in your garden. The space should hold anything that's meaningful to you.

"One of the purposes of ritual is to be an art of memory, to remind you of the things that matter," says Moore. "I think it's useful to have objects or images around you—I surround my world with paintings and sculptures."

Objects and images could include flowers, sacred books like the Bible, photographs of people you love, or artwork or depictions of nature or religious subjects—anything that evokes spiritual feeling. Moore says one of the objects with special meaning for him is a bronze statue of his namesake, Saint Thomas More.

These objects are not meant for worship—they are merely reminders. "In our home we have little altars, which have sacred objects on them that we've picked up over the years," says Dr. Dossey. "And every time we pass by it's a little reminder."

Aside from creating a single space for prayer or contemplation, it's also important to think of your entire home in a spiritual way. "We should appreciate the sacredness of the things around us—the sacredness of one's home, so that the home is not just a shelter but a sacred place," says Moore. "You can design and furnish your home so that it isn't just practical but that it conveys a sense of the sacredness of marriage, the family, and friendship."

{tending our own gardens}

How do we become more receptive to the spiritual?

"Self-care, self-care, self-care," says Elizabeth Gilbert, author of *Eat, Pray, Love: One Woman's Search for Everything Across Italy, India and Indonesia* and *Pilgrims*. While helping others is an essential part of being spiritual, we also have to see to our own needs. Neglecting ourselves sometimes can lead to emotional burnout. "I think people often don't include themselves in the host of the needy. Volunteering is a wonderful thing, but sometimes you need to allow yourself to sleep in on a Saturday or stay home from work, turn the telephone off, curl up with a cup of hot chocolate, and read a novel. These can also be pathways to the heart, but they're the hardest things for people to do because there is so much attendant guilt that goes with everything that's being neglected."

Gilbert says that you must be able to help yourself before you help others. "There's a story about an Indian guru who came to America. He was talking to this very frazzled mess of a woman—I say that affectionately having been that person—and he said to her, 'What do you want for your life?' And she said, 'I want to help others.' He answered her, 'But you haven't even done that for yourself yet—how can you help anybody?' So I would like to be a missionary for self-care, for gentleness and forgiveness toward ourselves in our spiritual journey." ⎘

Bibliography

Food and Nutrition

Bricklin, Mark, et al. *Prevention Magazine's Nutrition Advisor: The Ultimate Guide to the Health-Boosting and Health-Harming Factors in Your Diet.* Rodale, 1993.

Carper, Jean. *Food—Your Miracle Medicine: How Food Can Prevent and Cure over 100 Symptoms and Problems.* HarperCollins, 1993.

Duyff, Roberta Larson. *The American Dietetic Association's: Complete Food and Nutrition Guide.* John Wiley & Sons, 20 02.

Foods That Harm, Foods That Heal: An A–Z Guide to Safe and Healthy Eating. Reader's Digest, 1997.

Hyman, Mark. *Ultra-Metabolism: The Simple Plan for Automatic Weight Loss.* Scribner, 2006.

Nestle, Marion. *What to Eat: An Aisle-by-Aisle Guide to Savvy Food Choices and Good Eating.* North Point, 2006.

Pratt, Steven, and Kathy Matthews. *SuperFoods Rx: Fourteen Foods That Will Change Your Life.* HarperCollins Publishers, 2004.

Rinzler, Carol Ann. *Nutrition for Dummies, 4th ed.* John Wiley & Sons, 2006.

Sacks, Frank M., medical ed. *Healthy Eating: A Guide to the New Nutrition.* Harvard Medical School, 2006.

Somer, Elizabeth. *Food & Mood: The Complete Guide to Eating Well and Feeling Your Best.* Henry Holt, 1999.

————. *10 Habits That Mess Up a Woman's Diet.* McGraw-Hill, 2006.

Stampfer, Meir J., medical ed. *Vitamins and Minerals: What You Need to Know.* Harvard Medical School, 2006.

Willett, Walter C. *Eat, Drink, and Be Healthy: The Harvard Medical School Guide to Healthy Eating.* Free Press, 2001.

Zinczenko, David. *The Abs Diet: Eat Right Every Time Guide.* Rodale, 2005.

Sleep

Dement, William C., and Christopher Vaughan. *The Promise of Sleep: A Pioneer in Sleep Medicine Explores the Vital Connection Between Health, Happiness, and a Good Night's Sleep.* Dell, 1999.

Graber, Richard, with Paul Gouin. *How to Get a Good Night's Sleep: More Than 100 Ways You Can Improve Your Sleep.* Chronimed, 1995.

Idzikowski, Chris. *Learn to Sleep Well: A Practical Guide to Getting a Good Night's Rest.* Chronicle, 2000.

Jacobs, Gregg D. *Say Good Night to Insomnia: A Drug-Free Program Developed at Harvard Medical School.* Henry Holt, 1998.

Krugman, Michael. *The Insomnia Solution: The Natural, Drug-Free Way to a Good Night's Sleep.* Warner, 2005.

Kryger, Meir. *Can't Sleep, Can't Stay Awake.* HarperCollins, 2004.

Walsleben, Joyce A., and Rita Baron-Faust. *A Woman's Guide to Sleep: Guaranteed Solutions for a Good Night's Rest.* Crown, 2000.

Wolfson, Amy R. *The Woman's Book of Sleep: A Complete Resource Guide.* New Harbinger, 2001.

Exercise

American College of Sports Medicine. *ACSM Fitness Book: A Proven Step-by-Step Program from the Experts.* Human Kinetics, 2003.

Callahan, Lisa. *The Fitness Factor: Every Woman's Key to a Lifetime of Health and Well-Being.* Lyons, 2002.

Exercise: A Program You Can Live With. Harvard Medical School, 2002.

Moffat, Marilyn, and Carole B. Lewis. *Age-Defying Fitness: Making the Most of Your Body for the Rest of Your Life.* Peachtree, 2006.

Nelson, Miriam E., with Sarah Wernick. *Strong Women Stay Slim.* Bantam, 1998.

Schlosberg, Suzanne, and Liz Neporent. *Fitness for Dummies.* John Wiley & Sons, 2000.

Simon, Harvey B. *The No Sweat Exercise Plan: Lose Weight, Get Healthy, and Live Longer.* McGraw-Hill, 2006.

Health and Wellness

Boston Women's Health Book Collective. *Our Bodies, Ourselves: A New Edition for a New Era.* Touchstone, 2005.

Carlson, Karen J., Stephanie A. Eisenstat, and Terra Ziporyn. *The New Harvard Guide to Women's Health.* Harvard University Press, 2004.

Domar, Alice D., and Henry Dreher. *Healing Mind, Healthy Woman: Using the Mind-Body Connection to Manage Stress and Take Control of Your Life.* Dell, 1996.

———. *Self-Nurture: Learning to Care for Yourself As Effectively As You Care for Everyone Else.* Penguin, 2000.

Gordon, James S. *Manifesto for a New Medicine: Your Guide to Healing Partnerships and the Wise Use of Alternative Therapies.* Addison-Wesley, 1996.

Greene, Robert E., and Leah Feldon. *Dr. Robert Greene's Perfect Balance.* Three Rivers, 2005.

Nelson, Miriam E., with Sarah Wernick. *Strong Women, Strong Bones: Everything You Need to Know to Prevent, Treat, and Beat Osteoporosis.* Perigee, 2000.

Northrup, Christiane. *The Wisdom of Menopause: Creating Physical and Emotional Health and Healing During the Change.* Bantam, 2006.

———. *Women's Bodies, Women's Wisdom: Creating Physical and Emotional Health and Healing.* Bantam, 1994.

Roizen, Michael F., and Mehmet C. Oz. *You: The Owner's Manual: An Insider's Guide to the Body That Will Make You Healthier and Younger.* HarperResource, 2005.

Sobel, David S., and Robert Ornstein. *The Healthy Mind Healthy Body Handbook*. Time-Life Medical, 1996.

Weil, Andrew. *Eight Weeks to Optimum Health: A Proven Program for Taking Full Advantage of Your Body's Natural Healing Power*. Alfred A. Knopf, 2006.

———. *Healthy Aging: A Lifelong Guide to Your Well-Being*. Anchor, 2005.

Shelter and Safety

E/The Environmental Magazine, editors of. *Green Living: The E Magazine Handbook for Living Lightly on the Earth*. Plume, 2005.

Kanner, Catherine. *The Book of the Bath*. Fawcett Columbine, 1985.

Mendelson, Cheryl. *Home Comforts: The Art & Science of Keeping House*. Scribner, 1999.

Papolos, Janice. *The Virgin Homeowner: The Essential Guide to Owning, Maintaining and Surviving Your Home*. Penguin, 1997.

Mind

Campbell, Susan. *Getting Real: 10 Truth Skills You Need to Live an Authentic Life*. HJ Kramer/New World Library, 2001.

Fosdick, Harry Emerson. *On Being a Real Person*. Harper & Brothers, 1943.

Frankl, Viktor E. *Man's Search for Meaning*. Washington Square Press, 1959.

Hayes, Steven C., with Spencer Smith. *Get Out of Your Mind and into Your Life: The New Acceptance & Commitment Therapy.* New Harbinger, 2005.

Kabat-Zinn, Jon. *Wherever You Go There You Are: Mindfulness Meditation in Everyday Life.* Hyperion, 2005.

Langer, Ellen J. *Mindfulness.* Addison-Wesley, 1989.

McKay, Matthew, Martha Davis, and Patrick Fanning. *Thoughts and Feelings: Taking Control of Your Moods and Your Life.* New Harbinger, 1997.

Pelletier, Kenneth R. *Sound Mind, Sound Body: A New Model for Lifelong Health.* Fireside, 1995.

Saltz, Gail. *Becoming Real: Defeating the Stories We Tell Ourselves That Hold Us Back.* Riverhead, 2004.

Spirit

Caliandro, Arthur. *Make Your Life Count.* Harper & Row, 1990.

———. *Simple Steps: Ten Things You Can Do to Create an Exceptional Life.* McGraw-Hill, 2000.

Cameron, Julia. *The Vein of Gold: A Journey to Your Creative Heart.* Jeremy P. Tarcher/Penguin, 1996.

Chopra, Deepak. *How to Know God: The Soul's Journey into the Mystery of Mysteries.* Three Rivers, 2000.

Dossey, Larry. *The Extraordinary Healing Power of Ordinary Things: Fourteen Natural Steps to Health and Happiness.* Harmony, 2006.

Gilbert, Elizabeth. *Eat, Pray, Love: One Woman's Search for Everything Across Italy, India and Indonesia.* Viking, 2006.

Keating, Thomas. *Open Mind, Open Heart: The Contemplative Dimension of the Gospel*. Continuum, 2001.

Kushner, Harold S. *Living a Life That Matters: Resolving the Conflict Between Conscience and Success*. Alfred A. Knopf, 2001.

———. *Overcoming Life's Disappointments*. Alfred A. Knopf, 2006.

Moore, Thomas. *Care of the Soul: A Guide for Cultivating Depth and Sacredness in Everyday Life*. HarperCollins, 1992.

———. *The Soul's Religion: Cultivating a Profoundly Spiritual Way of Life*. Harper Perennial, 2003.

Thurman, Robert. *Infinite Life*. Riverhead, 2004.

Warren, Rick. *The Purpose Driven Life: What on Earth Am I Here For?* Zondervan, 2002.

Zukav, Gary. *The Seat of the Soul*. Fireside, 1989.

About the Author

DONNA WILKINSON is a journalist who writes about health and the arts. She has contributed to *The New York Times, InStyle, Self, Art & Antiques, Travel & Leisure, Traditional Home, Parents Magazine, Fitness,* and many other publications. She has also worked as an editor for several newspapers, magazines, and book publishers. She lives in New York City.